144

D0614834

Donated by

Dr. A. V. Henderson
Temple Baptist Church
Detroit, Mich

I Want To Enjoy My Children

ALSO BY DR. HENRY BRANDT . . .

I Want My Marriage to Be Better

I Want To Enjoy My Children

A Handbook on Parenthood

Dr. Henry Brandt / Phil Landrum

ZONDERVAN PUBLISHING HOUSE
OF THE ZONDERVAN CORPORATION
GRAND RAPIDS, MICHIGAN 49506

I WANT TO ENJOY MY CHILDREN

Copyright © 1975 by The Zondervan Corporation
Grand Rapids, Michigan

Fifth printing August 1977

Library of Congress Cataloging in Publication Data

Brandt, Henry R.
  I want to enjoy my children.

  1. Parent and child. 2. Family — Religious life.
I. Landrum, Phil, joint author. II. Title.
HQ772.B6815   261.8'342'7   75-21115

ISBN 0-310-2631-1

All Scripture   references from the New Testament are taken from *The New
International Version of the New Testament.* Copyright © 1973 by New York Bible
Society International. Used by permission.

All Scripture references from the Old Testament are taken from the *Revised
Standard Version.* Copyright 1952 and 1972 by the Division of Christian Education
of the National Council of Churches of Christ in the United States of America. Used
by permission.

Printed in the United States of America

Eva and I dedicate this book
to our children, Dick, Beth,
and Sue. It was fun raising
them, and we followed the
principles taught in this book.
The fellowship between us
continues to grow.

Contents

I Want To Enjoy My Children

1 / Enjoyable Parenthood

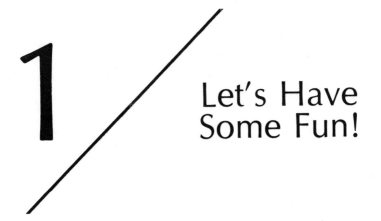

1 / Let's Have Some Fun!

1 / Let's Have Some Fun

The Dream/

It starts out as a dream. Doting, expectant fathers and their pregnant wives dream about the sweet little infant all cozy in pink and blue blankets with ribbons and talcum powder. With smiles in their eyes, they turn to each other and vow:

"We're going to be the best parents ever!"

Then the baby arrives. Suddenly the parents discover that "the dream" yells. And smells. And has a reversible stomach. All at 3 A.M.

It's enough to make a grown man cry — or even worse. I can remember taking our squalling baby and shoving it toward my wife, saying:

"You take it."

It's humbling to realize that what you thought were wonderful, parental instincts can't always be counted on when you need them.

Imagine a big man letting a tiny little baby get him angry! Yet it happens all the time.

The Nightmare/

One lady described to me a completely fruitless dialogue that had become an everyday occurrence at home with her thirteen-year-old son.

Mother: It's time to take out the garbage.

Son: (No response)

Mother: (Irritated) I said it's time to take out the garbage!

Son: O.K. (But still no movement)

Mother: (Angry and losing control) Well, don't just stand there! I said *Take out the garbage!*

Son: All right . . . all right.

Mother: (After a minute of seething silence and still no movement) *Take out the garbage! Now! Right now!*

Finally, the son stirs and goes through the evening ritual of taking out the garbage. As usual, he leaves one sack. Then he sits down again.

Mother: (Now screaming) *You stupid, rebellious kid! Get the rest of that garbage and take it out . . . and don't try to tell me you didn't see. . . .*

It's easy to see why the woman felt as she did when she came to my office.

"I just hate myself. I'm turning into a mess. I'm just nothing but a screaming, old nag of a mother."

I saw a similar situation at an airport. There, squeezed into a waiting-room chair, was an overly obese lady, with a tiny, squirming pre-schooler on her lap.

He wanted down. He finally wormed his way to the floor and headed toward the gate leading to the corridor. His mom called to him.

"You come back here."

The boy kept going.

"Did you hear me? I said come back here. Now!" she ordered, still entrenched in her chair. The boy moved his little legs faster than ever and scooted into the busy corridor.

From her chair, the mom fired several more commands after her disappearing son.

"If you don't come back here, you're going to get it." (No response)

"I'm going to come after you." (Still no response)

As the boy emerged across the hall in another

departure waiting area, the large lady threw out a few more threats — each completely ignored by the boy, who was now exploring the ticket counter across the hall. Finally, the lady gave up and slouched further down in her chair. She said, to no one in particular:

"I don't know what I'm going to do with that kid."

Obviously nothing. That "kid" was going to lead this great big mom on a lifelong merry chase, just as the other mom would be emotionally depleted over the daily garbage debate.

For these two mothers, parenthood won't be much fun. It won't be a challenge. It won't seem like the greatest profession on earth.

But it could be, just as it could be for anyone who reads this book. Parenthood can be a happy adventure, but there are principles that need to be followed.

A Dishful of Applesauce – Confident Expectation

One of the initial principles of successful and enjoyable parenthood is *confident expectation*. This assumes you are doing or requiring something you believe is worthwhile and is in the best interest of your child. If you are, you will have enough conviction to see it through.

When I did graduate work at Cornell University, the faculty did some experiments with different methods of helping children and parents. These were deftly done. One well-thought-out series involved mothers who could not control their children. The incidents were recorded on film and then shown to various classes.

I'll never forget the one about the mother who could not feed her son applesauce. Every time she tried, the boy shoved the spoon away. This was the cue for the mother to turn to the researcher and shrug.

"See? He just won't eat it."

The researcher told her to try again, which she did — unsuccessfully. Finally, the mother gave up.

"This happens all the time," she said.

Then one of the teachers tried it. She was determined in a gentle and firm way. She meant to feed that child applesauce — that was obvious.

17

The teacher put some applesauce on the spoon, headed it toward the child's mouth, and the child shoved it aside.

Without any hesitation, the teacher brought the spoon back and into the child's mouth.

Gulp! One spoonful of applesauce down the hatch. The child was surprised. The mother even more so.

The teacher did it again. This time the child was ready and pushed the spoon away, but the teacher again steadily returned the spoon back and around the little fist. Once more, the applesauce popped into the child's mouth.

Another surprised gulp. Now the child had two spoonfuls of applesauce in his stomach.

A third thrust with the spoon again succeeded. The fourth thrust went in without any resistance at all.

Soon the child was enjoying the applesauce more than the hitting. In no time at all the teacher had emptied the entire dish of applesauce — a spoon at a time — into the child's now willing mouth.

Why the difference? Confident expectation.

This the teacher explained to the stunned mother. It was a simple matter. The mother expected to fail. She was taking her cues from that little child. A little bit of resistance (which is normal in human beings) from the small child was enough to frustrate a grown woman.

In the next few sessions the mother watched the teacher successfully feed bowl after bowl of applesauce to her child. One thing was obvious in all the sessions. The teacher wasn't forcing the applesauce into the child's mouth just to prove a point. She wanted to do the child a favor. Her manner was friendly, gentle, and firm.

The teacher taught the mother that resistance is to be expected from children but that it can be overcome with gentle, well-founded pressure — pressure that is based on confident expectation.

After a few days of observing, the mother was urged to try again. The child took one look at the setup — the bowl of applesauce . . . the spoon . . . the mother. And it all came back to him. He knew his role in this drama. Resist.

But he was up against something different. This

time, the mother was dedicated to success. She was convinced she was doing the child a favor.

She took a spoonful of applesauce and headed it for the child. *Ah hah!* You could see the child's thinking mirrored on his face. He batted it away.

The mother brought it back. With a gleam in his eye, the child shoved it aside. This time she brought it back quicker than he expected and the spoonful of applesauce disappeared into his pouting mouth.

Gulp, indeed. The child couldn't believe his taste buds. The betrayed expression on his face was a sight to see.

And the mother's expression was incredible. You'd have thought she'd just inherited a million dollars. Her face was wreathed in a million-dollar glow of triumph.

She was victorious! She'd gotten a spoonful of applesauce into her child's mouth. Soon, the child sensed the difference, too. His mother's manner was friendly, gentle, and firm. Before the bowl was empty you had a mother feeding applesauce to a willing and cooperative child.

Remember that phrase . . . *confident expectation*. If you are to give your children the guidance they need, it will first of all take conviction on your part that you truly are doing your children a favor by what you are asking them to do.

Expect success. Parenthood will be a lot more fun.

Me . . . an Authority?

Success, however, implies being up on things. You can be the world's greatest authority on the subject of your children — if you pay attention to them.

And, of course, that's the catch. You must work at it — *talk* with them. *Listen* to them. *Play* with them. *Read* to them. *Pray* with them. *Work* with them.

Spend time with them.

Do it.

Become an authority on something. Rather, on someone — your children.

Socrates Said It . . .

Parents play a strategic role in society — to put it

more correctly, *the most strategic* role in society.

Consider this quotation from Socrates in 469 B.C.

> If I could get to the highest place in Athens, I would lift up my voice and say, "What mean ye fellow citizens that you turn every stone to scrape wealth together and take so little care of your children, *to whom you must one day relinquish it all?*"

Sounds like a modern statement, doesn't it? Isn't it true that by the time you do your job, get in some recreation, and carry out your social opportunities, it becomes difficult to find the time or the energy to pay enough attention to your children?

"Pass the Salt, Or I'll . . ."

If you spend a lot of time with your children, you'll learn a lot about them. Also a lot about yourself.

And you can always count on your children to pop the bubble — to shatter your polished image of yourself.

My wife and I still cringe with embarrassment when we recall the visit of our college president. It was quite an honor for a couple of young students to entertain the president, and we were determined to make the most of it.

The apartment looked as it had never looked before. Everything was in place, polished to a high luster. We were supposed to act as though it was always this way and carefully coached our little pre-school children on what they could and couldn't say. We practically wrote them a script, but how painfully we paid for the sham we were creating.

So the president came. We stumbled over ourselves to make him comfortable. We got him to the table all right and sat him next to our little daughter who had barely learned to talk. That was a mistake. (It's interesting to note how many mistakes you can make when you're trying to put up a front.)

During the meal this little tot said to the president in her bird-like voice:

"Will you please pass the salt?"

Nobody paid any attention. We were listening to the president. So she tried again.

20

"Will you please pass the salt?" A small, little voice that was easy to ignore as we strained at every word of the president.

But the third time this little curly-haired tot singlehandedly smashed all illusion about the offspring of the Brandt family we had so carefully constructed. She hammered our distinguished guest on the arm and yelled:

"Pass the salt or I'll knock your block off!"

I turned all shades of angry purple. The most palatable idea to me at that moment was to twist that little kid into a pretzel.

Yet there was no real reason to be angry. She had simply exposed my spirit — the spirit she had seen at previous meals. Also, we should have known we were expecting too much of a tiny child.

I've told this story all over the world and everyone thinks it's funny. Why didn't I think it was funny?

Wouldn't it be great if we could enjoy our experiences as much as we enjoy talking about them!

Under the Shadow of Death

I had no idea how tender a father could feel toward his child until our little Beth developed virus pneumonia and passed under the shadow of death.

She had been crying a lot in her playpen. I accused my wife of spoiling her, but she insisted our baby was ill. We agreed to let the doctor decide. His terrible diagnosis of virus pneumonia left us weak with fear.

At the time there was no known treatment. We left her alone in the hospital, went home to wait, and wait.

Not only would she not respond, but she also got to the place where she wouldn't eat. I stood helpless by the bedside of our little baby as she wasted away, and I then realized how much I loved that little youngster. A few days earlier I had been mad at her. Now with a heart filled with love there was nothing I wouldn't do for her. My wife and I clung to each other, desperately praying for the life of our baby. I asked God to forgive me for my impatience and lack of concern.

Day after day, I rushed from classes at the college

to be with my daughter. Still she wouldn't eat, so the attendants began feeding her intravenously. But she grew thinner and thinner.

One evening I asked the nurse if I could hold my little girl. That night Beth took some milk from the bottle as I held her in my arms.

She wouldn't eat for anyone else. Only I could feed her — I who had been angry with her for crying too much. I who had actually blocked taking her to a doctor because I thought she was being "spoiled."

Finally, she made it. The lesson: We need to know and respect our children.

One of the Pleasantest Tasks /

That was a long time ago, more than thirty years ago. You might say it's over for us, this matter of being parents. At least we've raised all our children to the point where they are out on their own.

I want to say that this is the stage I like the most. The children are gone.

I'm not saying that because we did not like the job. I am saying it because everyone of us who has children realizes that there is an element of suspense in raising them.

How will they turn out? It is a relief at this stage of the game to know that all three of our children have turned out quite well.

It's also a good time to write a book about raising children — after they're gone. It just so happens the principles in this book are the same ones we used when our children were still quite small.

These principles worked for us — and for thousands of parents who have consulted with me.

They made those years of close parenthood a pleasant time. And parenthood should be enjoyable, even during those years we fear the most. The teenage years, for example, can be the greatest of all.

Parenthood is not difficult. It is demanding. It takes time, some deep convictions, your own good example, some knowledge of your kids, following the teachings of the Bible, and a loving spirit.

22

Parents are strategic, important people, involved in one of the greatest adventures of life. You should never let go of that dream about being the best parents ever.

You can expect success — and also learn from your children. You should expect to grow, to change, to improve. No one is so bad off that his nightmare cannot be banished.

Most of all, parenthood should be an adventure. Come on, let's have a little fun.

2/ The Runaways

2 / The Runaways

Let's have fun. Expect success. Learning as you "parent." Meaningful relationships.

These are all good phrases, exciting ones. Also, they describe what every parent really wants. And they must be central to your adventure into enjoyable parenthood. But for a moment, let's digress. Let's look at some parents who aren't having fun.

Why get into the negative? Simple.

Because most parents aren't having fun.

One Promise /

Before you start this chapter, you have to make one promise. Don't condemn these unhappy parents. To realize the point of this chapter you have to be sympathetic with them. You can't be critical.

Two Men /

A successful author was quoted recently concerning his decision to leave his wife and six children:

"Part of me felt like a rat, but I had to ask myself if I could live there any longer, and I couldn't."

It was a question of freedom, he explained. "And I probably never again will be able to live with the impingements of marriage and parenthood."

An Academy-Award-winning actor expressed

somewhat the same sentiments in explaining why he left his twenty-year-old girl friend who was pregnant for the second time with one of his children.

"We're friends, but we're not living together any more. It was the only honest thing to do. I've never been able to pretend something that is not true.

"She's living with her folks. That's the best place to be when you're carrying a baby. . . .

"Children must not be allowed to complicate things, no matter how painful it might be to leave each other."

To say the least, the children involved will suffer. But they would also suffer if the marriage continued. It's certainly not a good situation for children to grow up in an atmosphere of discontent and conflict.

It is better for the children to let someone else create a better atmosphere for them. If the impingements of marriage and/or the complications of parenthood short circuit contentment, then it is better to remove the cause.

Interesting logic, isn't it? Remember now, you promised not to be critical. These men are not alone. They represent millions of couples who are highly literate, successful in other areas of their lives, and even maintain congenial personal relations outside the marriage.

Many brilliant, intelligent, successful people have concluded:

"To leave is best for the children. I'm no good for them. I'll just mess up their lives if I stick around."

The author and the actor represent the agonizing heartcry of millions of people in this country.

Any sensible couple starts out planning for their relationship to be the best ever. In all my years of counseling, I have never had one parent or set of parents come to me and say:

"Well, here we are, Dr. Brandt. We are bursting with mutual admiration because we've succeeded at reaching our goal. Our objective was to create an intolerable situation for the two of us —*and our children.*

"Now we've done it — created the perfect mess. We can't stand each other. We've ruined a good relationship — exactly what we started out to do."

Of course not. People just don't set such goals. Well, why is this marital upheaval in our society happening? Good people start marriage with the highest of hopes and the best of intentions and end up hopelessly at odds. The idea of personal freedom becomes an obsession and marriage and parenthood becomes a nightmare with no apparent solution.

The husband can't help himself to get out of his nightmare and in good conscience he feels he can no longer subject his children to the nightmare either.

So he quits, walks out on his kids. Women do this too. Couples didn't plan it that way. They didn't start out aiming for this situation. Having arrived, however, they don't know what else to do.

They have simply run out of ideas.

"I Sentence You to . . ."

To compound their plight, parenthood is a twenty-year process.

For some parents this is good news. For most, this is a scary thought. You mean I've got to put up with the screaming . . . the disobedience . . . the lack of respect . . . the rebellion for twenty years?

Is that all I have to look forward to?

Maybe. In any case, it is about twenty years per child. If you have more than one, it's that much longer.

Starts sounding like a sentence, doesn't it? Almost as if the gavel had slammed down and the judge had said: "I sentence you to twenty years in parenthood."

No wonder many people want to run away.

Morning Dialogue

Many parents attempt to deal with the problems by simply avoiding conflict. If there is a possible clash of opinions, they avoid it. After all, it's important to give our children the freedom to make their own decisions, isn't it? Consider:

A mother comes into her child's room in the morning, rouses her, and the following dialogue ensues:

29

Mother: Well, shall we get up today?

Child: No. (Child closes her eyes and burrows back
down under the covers.)

Mother: You have to get up to put your dress on. You do
want to get dressed, don't you?

Child: No. (Child snuggles down tighter than ever,
pulling a pillow over her head.)

Mother: You can eat breakfast after you put your dress
on. You'd like to do that, wouldn't you?

Child: (A sound emerges from underneath the pillow
that could be translated only as another No.)

Mother: After breakfast, you can watch TV. You'd like
that, wouldn't you?

Child: (No answer at all, now.)

And so it goes. Every morning this mother goes
through the same twenty-minute nerve-wracking ritual as
she cajoles her child into getting up for another day. The
mother does this for the one simple reason that she wants to
avoid conflicts in life. And forcing a child to do certain
things results in conflicts and resistance.

Parents go through a similar agony in other situations, passing along the decisions to the child:

Shall we make our bed and pick up our room?
Shall we eat breakfast? Shall we drink our milk? Shall we go
to school? Aren't you staying out too late? Aren't you
running with the wrong crowd?

And the daily fight is on.

"Chris Is Driving Me Nuts"

These situations reveal persistent unhappiness.
"Christopher gets me down! He's driving me nuts," says a
mother. "Today I turned my back on him for a moment and
he was gone.

"I had to get everyone in the neighborhood out
looking for him. We finally found him at a playground.

"He keeps me in a constant turmoil. If only he'd be
good I'd be happy."

That was a young mother talking. A sixty-year-old
lady told of a similar feeling of unhappiness that had fol-

30

lowed her all her life. Her life was a series of lifelong tragedies.

Not only did she have an alcoholic husband and a shaky marriage, but all four of her children had troublesome marriages of their own. Her heartbreak was being multiplied four times.

And her husband was no help.

Unhappiness . . . it's everywhere among parents.

A Little More Sympathy?

Getting the picture? Are you a little more sympathetic now toward those real, live people who stand behind the divorce statistics? Can you begin to sense their dilemma?

Would you be happy with a twenty-year sentence of unhappiness, of daily conflict, and of ultimate guilt when faced with the truth that you might not be capable of even being a good example for your children?

A Poem About Sheep

During my family life lectures, I have used what I always believed to be an inspirational poem. Gradually, however, I've come to realize the poem is a rebuke to many, rather than an inspiration. Read it.

It was a sheep — not a lamb, that strayed
In the parable Jesus told:
A grown-up sheep that had gone away
From the ninety and nine in the fold.

Out in the meadows out in the cold,
'Twas a sheep the Good Shepherd sought:
Back to the flock, and into the fold,
'Twas a sheep the Good Shepherd brought.

And why, for the sheep, should we earnestly long,
And so earnestly hope and pray?
Because there is danger, if they go wrong;
They will lead the young lambs astray.

For the lambs will follow the sheep, you know,
Wherever the sheep may stray
If the sheep go wrong, it will not be long
'Til the lambs are as wrong as they.

So, with the sheep we earnestly plead,
For the sake of the lambs today:
If the lambs are lost, what a terrible cost
Some sheep may have to pay.

— *Author Unknown*

Who really can stand to take the incredible responsibility set out in the poem about sheep? It's pretty frightening.

So what options do we have? It's understandable that the divorce applications now almost equal the marriage applications.

Are we perpetrating a hoax by saying that parenthood ought to be a lot of fun? Is that unrealistic? A pie-in-the-sky suggestion?

I guess one thing we can agree on — parenthood definitely will bring out the worst in us. And we don't like what we see. At the office we can look good most of the time. In the club or other organization we can appear pretty much in control. You can't pretend twenty-four hours a day. So parenthood won't let you hide the worst side of yourself.

It's scary. We'd rather not be reminded of it. That's why we run. We don't want to stick around these kids for five . . . ten . . . fifteen more years and see our faults mirrored in their lives.

A Better Way

The question is: How do you get to the place where you don't have to run away? There must be a better way. In the next chapters, we'd like to offer you a better way — some alternatives. We want to give you some more ideas.

3 / A Place to Start

3/ A Place to Start

The Quick Reverse

A swimming teacher was describing how to properly rescue a drowning person. As I listened I was fascinated by the little-known precautionary step called *the quick reverse.*

"The *quick reverse*," said the teacher, "is used when the rescuer comes close to the victim, which is the moment of greatest potential danger.

"A drowning victim is desperate and irrational. If he can, he will grab the lifesaver, immobilize, or even drown him.

"A good *quick reverse* stops the rescuer's momentum before he gets hopelessly — and fatally — trapped. It also moves the lifesaver out of the victim's reach.

"The lifesaver doesn't abandon the victim. The *quick reverse* enables the rescuer to calmly study the victim, approach the victim safely, take charge, and tow him to safety.

"A knowledgeable rescuer does not panic, regardless of the victim's behavior. He takes command, acts decisively (even if the victim struggles against him), and helps the victim reach a common goal: SAFETY.

"A good lifesaver is not afraid of people in trouble. It's his job to rescue them. It gives him satisfaction.

"Nor does a good lifesaver dive in every time he

sees someone struggling. He doesn't tamper with the child who is just learning how to swim and struggling along the side of the pool. It is important for that child to be allowed to work on the problem himself.

"A good lifesaver gets involved only when there's trouble brewing. He has to be calm, happy, cooperative, able, under control, and trained.

"If he is not, a crisis situation will cause him to panic. He might run away from it, completely deserting the pool he has agreed to guard. Or he might swim out and realize he is incapable of rescue and let the victim sink.

"Or he might swim right into the arms of danger, get grabbed by the victim and end up part of a double drowning."

No One Plans to Drown

To some of us, the teacher's speech may seem highly technical. But notice how it parallels parenthood. Just like the swimmers at a pool, children in a family situation are looking for fun out of life . . .pleasure . . . fellowship . . . good health.

Yet sometimes they get into trouble. Just like the swimmer who gets in trouble, the child doesn't plan to drown. He simply lacks knowledge. Or maybe he's unprepared, lacks ability or training, ignores obvious dangers, or disobeys the rules.

Regardless, when a child is drowning in life's problems, he needs to be rescued. He needs a capable "lifesaver" to come after him and tow him to safety. He needs a parent who is ready to move in at the first sign of danger.

Yet, many children aren't rescued. Their parents are in no position to help. They are out of control themselves, have no plan, or also are sinking.

Untrained parents are in a position of weakness and are trapped in a never-ending series of crises. They seem unable to change their direction and have no idea of any alternatives — except maybe to run off and get a divorce and let their children "drown." Otherwise, they'd drown too.

36

Their lives need a quick reverse.

Short-Lived Vow

No serious parent wakes up in the morning planning to make his child's life miserable. No parent vows each morning: "Today, I'm going to be grumpy, crabby, and impossible."

Can you imagine approaching parenthood with this attitude? Imagine you're in a maternity waiting room with an expectant father. Suddenly the father-to-be looks up at the ceiling and says with a strong tinge of iron-willed determination:

"Boy-oh-boy, is this baby going to regret having me as a father. I'm going to draw on all the ingenuity and creativity possible to make this little tyke's life utterly miserable."

No. It doesn't work that way. When the alarm goes off, it's just the opposite.

"Today will be different," the mother vows. "A great day. No screaming — impatient orders — arguing."

As Mom is making her vow, a situation is developing that will easily crush that well-meaning vow. In the hall outside the bathroom, her son is beating on the door.

"Hey, who's in there? You've been tying up the bathroom for half an hour. Do you think you're the only one who has to go to school?"

"Oh, buzz off!" comes the answer from big sister. "If you want to use the bathroom, why don't you go down in the basement and use the bathroom down there?"

"Why should I always have to be the one who uses the basement bathroom? Come on, now, open up. Now! Or I'll tell Mom!" This threat is accompanied by a drum roll on the door. Just then Mother comes on the scene.

She finds herself in the middle of a battle between a child who wants to use the bathroom and another who has locked herself in.

It doesn't take her long to get into the controversy. Several screams, protestations, and mutterings later she's settled the controversy. But she's irritated and upset.

Yet . . . only minutes before . . . she had vowed that this would be a perfect day.

Often it's the same for the well-intentioned dad. Just before he pulls into the driveway coming home from work, he vows:

"Tonight I'm not going to be a grouch. Tonight I'm going to have fun with the family."

But suddenly he finds his way blocked by two bicycles parked in the driveway, in spite of his many lectures against such a situation.

He parks the car, the engine running, halfway in the driveway and halfway in the street, slams the door, and runs toward the house.

Dad is hardly in the door before he's after everyone in sight.

"How many times do I have to tell you guys . . . *Get those bicycles out of the driveway!* How am I going to park the car?"

He's out of control — just making noise without getting any facts. He continues yelling, turning now on his wife. Without one loving gesture or question, he lays her out too:

"I thought I made it clear that bicycles should not be parked in the driveway." And the fight is on . . .

The mom at breakfast . . . the father coming home from work. Both found themselves in a crisis situation.

But they blew the rescue, didn't they?

The Possible Dream/

What we are looking for is the cause of the awful feelings and unbelievable behavior experienced around your partner and children — the people you want to love and be decent toward.

In other words, you've missed the mark.

What mark?

In the consulting room everyone expresses the same basic longings, the same goals — or mark — that all are shooting for:

1. To *enjoy* life every day.
2. Obtain *peace* which will keep your thoughts and hearts quiet and at rest.

3. Increase in *love* toward one another.

4. Be *unselfish* and *considerate*.

Would you be surprised if I told you that this is not an impossible dream? These attributes can characterize your life. They don't represent some distant, unreachable oasis.

Are you interested?

Watch Out!

We're about to examine the problem, the cause, and cure for your unhappiness.

But first — a warning!

I've watched many people explode with rage when I tried to explain the reasons for their behavior. I mention this only to warn you ahead of time that my answer comes from a source you may have rejected: the Bible.

"Don't give me that Bible stuff!" shouted one of my clients. "I've had that crammed down my throat ever since I was a kid."

Yet, after listening to what the Bible said, he saw his life turned around. He followed steps that have meant new life and happy parenthood for many.

For example, did you know that what you want for yourself (joy, peace, love, unselfishness, being considerate) is described in the Bible as God's will for you?

Still with me?

Good. Here we go. Let's start with the first questions . . . Why do I act the way I do? Why do I miss the mark?

The Mysterious Stranger

The problem. The Bible describes your condition in two lines:

> For what I do is not the good I want to do; no, the evil I do not want to do — this I keep on doing (Rom. 7:19).

Isn't this the problem? Everyone misses the mark. Maybe you're one of the many who vowed that your marriage would be the greatest. Now you'd settle for getting through breakfast without a squabble.

You can't control yourself, can you?

Cause. There is a mysterious stranger within you who won't behave as you intend to behave. The Bible which describes the problem also provides a cause:

> Now if I do what I do not want to do, it is no longer I who do it, but it is sin living in me that does it (Rom. 7:20).

Whoops!/

Did I use the wrong word there? It's an ugly word, all right. Before you dismiss it, think a minute. If I had said *virus* or *cancer*, you would listen. So, let's take another look at this definition of sin:

> For what I do is not the good I want to do; no, the evil I do not want to do — this I keep on doing (Rom. 7:19).

Can you improve on this description of yourself? It's an accurate description, even though you don't like the word *sin*. Don't get hung up on the word and miss some very important truths.

"What Do You Mean . . . ?"/

> There is no one who does good, not even one (Rom. 3:12).

"What do you mean, I've never done any good? I've done a lot of good in my life," you say.

And you're right. You have had many happy moments with your wife and children. You have been generous to others. And you continue to be.

That's not the problem. If you were in a fit of temper or resentment or selfishness, no one could make you do today what you did for them yesterday. This is the problem.

Suddenly . . . Enemies!/

Cynthia and her brother, Frank, had always been close. They were helpful neighbors and gave freely of their time and money to the church.

Then their parents died — and the will was read.

Cynthia was outraged. The will announced she was getting no more than the rest of the family, even though she had taken mother and father into her home and looked after them in their last years.

Frank just shrugged it off.

"A will is a will," he said, not about to concede. Neither was she. Suddenly, two people who had been close for a lifetime were enemies. She wouldn't speak to him. They'd meet at church, and she'd turn away when she saw him coming. This went on for over a year.

Here was a generous woman and a usually agreeable man who had been lifelong friends. Now they were being driven by selfishness, stubbornness, and hostility.

Both Frank and Cynthia still do a lot of good things. It's not the good deeds that divide them. It's *the good they do not do.* Both agree that selfishness, stubbornness, and hostility are not good. They say the will caused the problem. This is particularly ironic since neither of them need the money. The will revealed their spirits.

What sticks out? All the good things they've done? No. Their stubbornness, hostility, and selfishness.

Similar behavior is evident in all people. It's *sin.* It's *the good you do not do.* We're all in the same boat.

"No Wonder This Kid Has Diaper Rash!"

Consider the father starting out the day vowing to be a good husband and father. He wants to be a good parent. He pictures himself pulling into the driveway that night, friendly, responsible, patient, kind, and gentle.

But when he walks into the house there is no one to greet him. Worse yet, the baby is screaming — unattended. He goes to the crib and finds that the baby's diaper is soaked.

"Dirty, smelly diaper. No wonder the baby's crying," he mutters, storming out of the baby's room and slamming the door, eyes searching angrily for his obviously irresponsible wife.

What he doesn't realize — because he came in the garage door — is that his wife had a terrible headache that day. A short time earlier, she had laid down in the family room to give her pounding head a little rest and had dozed off.

The noise of a door shutting wakes her up — and the baby too. She gathers herself together and goes to the front door. But her husband has come in from the garage, gone through the kitchen, and directly into the adjacent bedroom for the baby.

The wife finds no one at the door. Surprised, she figures she's hearing things and goes quickly to the baby's room to take care of her crying child who has just awakened.

Just as she nears the baby's door, she meets her irate husband.

"Where have you been?" he storms. "No wonder this kid's got diaper rash! She never gets changed. You probably haven't changed her all day."

The wife, sick, tired, and spent from trying to do a full day's work in spite of her physical condition, breaks into tears. Between sobs, she spits out:

"You don't even know what you're talking about."

"I know one thing, you can bet on that," he fires back. "I go to work and face incredible problems all day long. You've got only one baby to take care of all day. What do I find when I come home? The place is a wreck, the baby's screaming, and you're off somewhere doing only God knows what."

This man and his wife didn't plan, or want such a scene.

Is the wife the cause of her husband's irritation? Did the husband cause his wife's irritation? Or was it her headache? Maybe the baby caused it all. Or perhaps someone else.

We are all sunk if peace of mind depends upon someone else's choices, behavior, or moods.

Are this man and wife doing anything that everyone else hasn't done in life? No, we're all in the same boat. We find ourselves powerless to exude joy, peace, gentleness in the face of a yelling husband, a pouting wife, bathroom fights, bicycles in the driveway, smelly diapers, or squalling babies.

The Joy Machine Is Missing /

So you don't have a joy machine that kicks in when you need it like your air conditioner does? Don't be dismayed. You are not alone. This is how the Bible has described us for centuries. Marriage and parenthood just bring the condition out more dramatically.

At this point you may be thinking, *I've got marriage and family problems, and now he makes me out a sinner, too. This just compounds my problem with guilt.*

Granted. The diagnosis of sin may startle or even frighten you. It's like hearing your physician tell you an operation is needed. You are stunned, afraid, unbelieving. You wish it would go away.

The physician does not give you the news to complicate your problems. His objective is to heal you, to correct something wrong. You are not functioning as you should — or would — because you are sick.

My goal for you is also your healing. The diagnosis of sin may be repulsive, frightening. But you are not functioning as you should — or would — because you are sinful. Don't let the diagnosis scare you. There is a cure.

The Cure /

God has a plan to save you from yourself, from your sins. You have everything to gain and nothing to lose from Him. The Bible says God will do for you what you cannot do for yourself. For instance:

> May the Lord make your love increase and overflow for each other and for everyone else, just as ours does for you (1 Thess. 3:12).

This is what you're looking for. Let God give you what He has promised. Your reactions toward your partner and your children will change. The Bible which describes the problem and defines the cause also spells out a solution:

> What a wretched man I am! Who will rescue me from this body of death? Thanks be to God — through Jesus Christ our Lord! (Rom. 7:24,25).

This is a name that sometimes makes people see red — Jesus Christ. People sometimes associate Him with unreasonable demands, punishment, guilt. But let Him speak for Himself.

> For God did not send his Son into the world to condemn the world, but to save the world through him (John 3:17).

Saved from what? Your nastiness, of course. Your sins. A sinner is like a traffic violator who has broken a traffic law. Nothing can change the fact that he is a violator. We have all experienced the sense of relief when we get out of a twenty mph traffic zone when we were traveling at forty mph.

You feel the same tension when you miss a mark of your own. You are vaguely aware of violating something, but what do you do about it? You must cure your problem through Jesus Christ. It is said of Him:

> . . . you are to give him the name Jesus, because he will save his people from their sins (Matt. 1:21).

It is Jesus who said:

> I am the way — and the truth and the life. No one comes to the Father except through me (John 14:6).

> Here am I! I stand at the door and knock, If anyone hears my voice and opens the door, I will go in and eat with him, and he with me (Rev. 3:20).

How, then, do you approach God?

1. *You start by recognizing that missing the mark is sin.* You agree with God. Your sins have separated you from Him.

2. *Next comes faith.* There is only one way to approach God and that is to try it. Choose to believe in God and act on that belief.

3. *Trust Jesus as your Savior.* You can do this right now through prayer (prayer is talking with God). Here is a suggested prayer:

> "Lord Jesus, I need You. I open the door of my life and receive You as my Savior and Lord. Thank You for forgiving my sins. Take control of my life. Make me the kind of person You want me to be."

4. *Confess your sins.* "But If we confess our sins to

him, he can be depended on to forgive us and to cleanse us from every wrong" (1 John 1:9, *Living Bible*).

That's no big deal. It's like, "Oops. I'm going forty in a twenty mph zone. So I'll acknowledge the fact that I'm violating a law and need to change. I'll simply take my foot off the accelerator and ask God for forgiveness."

Of course, repentance is involved. You've changed your mind about being a violator. You agree with the sign that you are violating a rule. This is what confession is. You admit you are wrong and plan to change.

When you do this, Jesus will forgive you and cleanse your life of those uncontrollable habits.

Why not try it? God can change your reactions to life. He can give you the resource you need. This is the quick reverse. This is the first step to enjoyable parenthood. Repeat step 4 as often as necessary.

Perhaps you are a Christian, but you have neglected step 4. List your sins and bring them to God. He will forgive you and clean you up.

Quick Reverse "Backlash"

One word of caution for you who decide you need a quick reverse and have decided to make a permanent relationship with Jesus Christ your first step to enjoyable parenthood.

That caution: expect your partner and/or children to be confused if you suddenly reverse your life.

A business friend of mine recently took the same step you have just taken. Noticing a difference in his life, his wife asked him what had happened. When he said he had asked Jesus Christ to take charge of his life, she shook her head and muttered:

"Religion, eh? You'll get over it. It was the American Legion last year . . . the Boy Scouts the year before . . . it's just another one of your little excursions."

This is a natural reaction. Expect it. Give your family six months to be skeptical. And don't try to overwhelm them with your new approach to life. Just let it be natural.

They'll get the point.

45

II / Parenthood As a Business

4 / Partners, Not Opponents

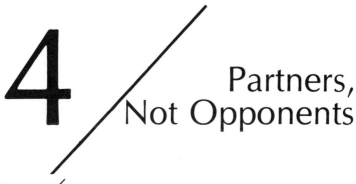

4 / Partners, Not Opponents

Partners/

Doesn't the word "partners" have a pleasant ring to it?

It reminds me of some other nice words: harmony . . . together . . . cooperation . . . agreement . . . appreciation . . . respect . . . success.

Any partnership is entered into with high hopes. It is hoped the partners will combine their resources, talents, and abilities, and will experience satisfaction and success in the process.

Can you imagine people who hate each other, don't trust one another, or who know ahead of time that they can't get along forming a partnership?

Can you imagine several people forming a partnership for the purpose of lying, cheating, and fighting with each other?

Can you imagine a partnership being formed with the hope that somewhere along the line the individuals involved will take each other to court and end up as frustrated enemies? This *is* done, of course. But who would say this is a sensible reason for forming one?

Obviously for a partnership to succeed, it takes honest people of good will who anticipate pleasant, happy relationships as they work together toward a common goal.

It is easy to understand a business partnership. For

51

example, four men agree to form a partnership to build some apartment houses. Between them, they must achieve the following:

1. A credit rating good enough to get money.
2. A set of building plans.
3. Acquire property.
4. Construct the building.
5. Manage the building.
6. Handle the income.

This is not a complete list, but it shows that a partnership requires resources, talent, cooperation, agreement. Assuming honest men of good will, the project should give them a great deal of satisfaction and a sense of success. In biblical language, it goes like this:

> Then make my joy complete by being like-minded, having the same love, being one in spirit and purpose. Do nothing out of selfish ambition or vain conceit, but in humility consider others better than yourselves (Phil. 2:2,3).

It is a simple matter to form a partnership. Making it achieve its objective is not so simple. That takes a lot of hard work. To do it in the spirit described in these Bible verses is a miracle.

Parenthood Is a Partnership

Obviously, the purpose of parenthood is to raise mature, happy, useful adults. Parents may be in the business voluntarily or involuntarily. No matter. The children are there. They won't dissolve. So the parents' task is to combine their own resources, talents, ability, and personalities to accomplish the chosen goal. And their objective, in biblical terms, is:

> Train up a child in the way he should go, and when he is old he will not depart from it (Prov. 22:6).

This is a formidable task to say the least and surely requires honest partners of good will giving the job their best efforts. It seems to me that in comparison to building apartments, raising children is an enormously more difficult and challenging objective.

It demands the utmost of cooperation between

parents over a twenty-year haul. Obviously, the first step is to accept the challenge and be committed to succeed together.

The One Big Hangup

In my consulting room I've listened to thousands of sad stories about strains in business partnerships, friendships, marriage, and parenthood. Assuming good will, friendship, and common goals to start with, most of the strains boil down to one major issue — *decision making*.

What is involved in decision making? The process is the same whether it's business, friendship, or parenthood.

The Cabinet Makers

Alvin and Roberto are equal partners in a custom kitchen cabinet shop. Both have the same amount of money invested, receive the same salary, and share equally in the profits. Alvin is president and general manager.

In addition to being responsible for the whole operation, he is specifically responsible for financing, cost control, paying bills, and advertising.

Roberto is sales manager and is responsible for installation. He can sell all the cabinets they can produce and does a great job of installation and keeping the customers happy. Alvin and Roberto have a happy, satisfying, and enjoyable partnership. Now listen in on a business meeting.

Alvin, Roberto, and the shop foreman, Ralph, who is an employee, are in the meeting.

> *Alvin* : Our planer machine is breaking down too often lately and isn't doing a smooth job.
>
> *Ralph* : That's right. It slows us down and makes extra work.
>
> *Roberto* : I agree. Some of our delivery dates aren't met and the customers don't like it.
>
> *Alvin* : Fine. I'll leave it to the two of you to choose another machine . . .O.K.?
>
> *Ralph/Roberto:* O.K.

Later, Ralph and Roberto got together to choose a machine. But they got hung up. Ralph recommended a new machine, and Roberto was sold on a used one which was bigger and cheaper.

A week later, Alvin called a meeting to find out what machine the other two men had decided to buy.

Alvin: Well, fellas, what did you decide?
(Silence)
Alvin: (To Roberto) What did you buy?
Roberto: We didn't buy anything.
Alvin: You didn't buy anything?
(Silence)
Alvin: What's wrong here?

To state the obvious, two hardworking friends became hung up on a decision. Now the question: how do you decide what to buy when all the facts are in, everything that can be said has been said, and you still differ?

I know of only one difficult way — *someone must have the last word.* But who?

In this partnership, Roberto and Alvin had agreed that Alvin would be the president of the partnership. Part of the president's job was to break stalemates.

His position was not a result of age, education, seniority, or investment. When the two men formed the partnership they simply agreed that Alvin was the one to have the last word. It was their choice — an act of will.

So Alvin was to have the last word in this case, even though when it came to machines he was the least qualified of the three to decide.

What would you have done if you had been Alvin? Probably the same as he did. He listened to each of the two men and gathered what other information he could. There was no clear-cut answer.

So he decided that since both of the partners had confidence in Ralph, and since Ralph was running the shop, he would go along with Ralph's recommendation.

Everyone accepted the decision, for they were men of good will, with faith in each other. Interestingly enough, the opinion taken was from the one who wasn't even a partner.

Now look in on another meeting.

Marie and Joe /

Joe and Marie are sitting in their living room. Joe is about to break some good news to his wife.

Joe: I just got a $100 per month raise. Let's invest it in a new couch.

Marie: You got a raise?! Hooray!
(They melt into each other's arms and after a few friendly hugs and kisses, they resume the conversation.)

Marie: A new couch would be great, Joe. This one is looking pretty tired.

Joe: It sure is. Let's go look at some in the store.
(After some silence)

Marie: Joe . . . ?

Joe: I'm listening. (He gives her a big hug.)

Marie: When we go to my mom's house, it's sure great to shove the dishes in a dishwasher. One of those would save me lots of work. (Pause) Let's get a dishwasher instead of a couch.
(There's a long silence.)

Marie: Joe? What are you thinking?

Joe: Why do you always contradict me? You know there's no room for a dishwasher in the kitchen. Besides, a couch will benefit the entire family, including you. Do we always have to differ over what to buy?

Marie: You don't have to get mad!

Joe: I'm not mad!

Well, Joe and Marie got hung up and their conversation over his raise ended in icy silence.

The next morning breakfast was a distasteful, uncomfortable, silent ordeal. It was a relief to both of them when Joe left for work.

That evening the air had cleared, supper was pleasant, and after the children were in bed, Joe and Marie had another meeting.

Joe: I'm sorry about my attitude last night.

Marie: Me too.

(They melt into each other's arms. For a moment, there is no conversation.)

Joe: I've been thinking. I thought we could price a dishwasher and a couch.

Marie: That's plenty fair enough.

They went shopping. They found out that a dishwasher wouldn't fit in the kitchen. Couches were more expensive than they thought. The old one would do a few years. The children were small and had a tendency to jump on the couch and even accidentally spill things on it. A new couch would be more of a problem at this time than a pleasure.

Isn't it strange what happens to friends? But sensible people will come up with reasonable decisions.

That Mysterious Stranger

Remember that mysterious stranger within? You find yourself feeling, thinking, saying, and doing the strangest things.

Why?

In the business, all three men wanted their business to succeed and they wanted to work together harmoniously. Yet, they got hung up over a decision. Joe and Marie had every intention of having a happy marriage, but ended up in cool silence over a decision.

Why?

Because of the nature of people. Remember the description of people in the last chapter?

> For what I do is not the good I want to do; no, the evil I do not want to do — this I keep on doing (Rom. 7:19).

Whenever two or more people must cooperate, no matter how dedicated, cooperative, or hard-working, they will sooner or later get hung up over a decision. They will come to a stalemate. Everything that could be said has been said. All the facts are in. There is nothing to be added. Still, they are hung up. But they don't intend to be.

A Matter of Opinion – But Whose?

Decision making reveals another side of human nature. The Bible describes it this way:

56

> All we like sheep have gone astray; we have turned every one to his own way; and the Lord has laid on him the iniquity of us all (Isa. 53:6).

How true. My ideas, my plans, my way of doing it sounds pretty good to me. So does yours to you. The businessmen and the marriage partners were all committed to harmonious relations. Yet, they found themselves straying away from that commitment because personal judgment seemed better than someone else's.

The choice of a machine, of a dishwasher vs. a couch, is *all a matter of opinion.* There is no right or wrong choice.

But whose opinion? The answer to this question is the key to successful partnerships.

Success in business, cooperation in marriage and parenthood — neither of these are lofty enough objectives to overcome the strong pull a person feels to go his own way, to do his own thing. "To do it my way" is the sweetest music to anyone's ears. So what do you do about this tendency? Here are some suggestions:

1. You admit the truth about yourself ("I want my own way").

2. You confess it to the Lord.

3. You ask Him to cleanse you and to give you a spirit of cooperation. Here is a suggested prayer — remember that prayer is talking to God — to help you make those steps:

> Dear Lord, I need Your help. My desire to push my own ideas drives me so hard it tends to spoil my fellowship with other people. I recognize this drive within me and I need Your help to correct it. Give me a spirit of cooperation.

Who Has the Last Word?

How do you solve the hangups in the cabinet shop and the living room?

First is personal preparation. Each person involved in the decision needs a God-given spirit of cooperation.

Second, each person involved is committed to reaching the objectives of the partnership.

57

Third, someone is designated in advance to *have the last word.* In a business it's the president. And in parenthood, it's . . . .

It's who . . . . . ?

The Most Controversial Question/

The answer to that question is one of the most controversial issues of our time. Marriages break up over this issue. Let's look in once more on Joe and Marie to see how they handled this matter of decision making.

At first, their discussion about a couch vs. a dishwasher ended up in icy silence. The question was not settled that night. It didn't need to be. Few questions require an immediate decision.

And an icy silence isn't the best way to end a discussion, either. But it happened. After all, we aren't talking about angels. Joe and Marie are people who tend to fight for their own way, like anyone else.

This isn't the first time these people got hung up over a decision. In fact they almost separated once because decisions piled up on them and the answers became a contest instead of a cooperative effort.

Fortunately, they ran into someone who introduced them to Jesus Christ. Jesus is now their Savior. They are learning to use the Bible to find clues on how to effectively live together. Also, they ask Jesus to help them.

The Controversial Answer/

They found a clue out of the Bible that saved their marriage. It was the answer to the most loaded of all questions — who has the last word? They found the clue when they were furious with each other over some basic issues. They both worked at the time, and these issues had stacked up:

Who makes the bed?
Who sweeps the floor?
Who washes dishes?
A red car or a blue car?
What speed do you drive on the freeway?
(She said sixty; he said seventy.)

58

Their friend who introduced them to searching the Bible for clues, led them to what they thought was a bombshell.

The question was: How do you solve a hangup? *The biblical answer was:*

> Wives, submit to your husbands as to the Lord. For the husband is the head of the wife as Christ is the head of the church, his body, of which he is the Savior (Eph. 5:22, 23).

Wowie!

When she read that, Marie hit the ceiling.

"I'm not taking orders from him," she said.

"Why not?" asked the friend.

"All he cares about is himself."

Marie was right. Of course, all *she cared* about was herself too. There is no way to succeed in a partnership between two people who are mad at each other and have no intention of cooperating. They hadn't intended to square off and oppose each other when they married, but they hadn't reckoned with that fact about human nature as described in Isaiah 53:6:

> All we like sheep have gone astray; we have turned every one to his own way; and the Lord has laid on him the iniquity of us all.

What is the iniquity of us all? My *judgment must prevail.* In other words, it's first of all a matter of spirit.

Joe and Marie decided to try it the Bible way. And they didn't stop with just that one controversial passage. There are some great ideas in Ephesians 5 that are quite palatable.

1. Don't be drunk with wine.
2. Be filled with the Spirit.
3. Have a song on your lips toward God
4. Have a melody in your heart toward God.
5. Have a thankful spirit toward God.
6. Be subject to one another in the fear of God.
7. Wives, be subject to your husbands as unto the Lord.
8. Husbands, love your wives and give yourself to

them. Love them as you do your own bodies —
as Christ loved the church.

Joe and Marie had the above points as their objectives. Yet, their conversation about buying a couch ended up in an icy silence.

What made the happy ending possible?

During the day both Joe and Marie separately realized each had drifted away from a God-given spirit of cooperation. Personal opinion had become more important than the partnership.

What do you do then? You repent, ask God to forgive and cleanse you, and return to your commitment. This made a friendly conversation possible that evening and resulted ultimately in a sensible decision about the growing problem.

It Saves Marriages

When honesty and good will prevail, most decisions will be settled in a mutually agreeable fashion. When there is a stalemate, someone must have the last word.

Joe and Marie decided to try the biblical way. It saved their marriage. When there is a stalemate, Joe settles it.

They still drift back to their old way of fighting over a decision, but when they realize what's happening, they return to the biblical way.

Does this idea make you see red?

Does it infuriate you?

Why does it? If the Bible is true, isn't it worth considering?

Try it.

Our next two chapters will give you some tips on working together as partners. So read on and this matter of having the last word will make more sense.

You will find being in business for yourself can be a lot of fun.

5 / Now . . . Heeeeerrrrre's Dad!

5 / Now . . . Heeeeerrrrre's Dad!

Dad Sets the Tone

Betty, age thirty-six, is speaking. "If there is one scene that I look forward to every day, it's when my husband Bob comes home from work.

"Sometimes the kids get to him in the driveway first. Sometimes we all see him at once as he comes through the door. But no matter how many times we've gone through it, his arrival always picks up the day for the rest of us.

"Maybe we've had a bad day. Maybe it's been a good day. In either case, when he pops through that door full of enthusiasm, sometimes with kids hanging all over him, I feel like saying, just like they do on the talk shows:
'Now . . . Heeeeerrrrre's Dad!'

The Prosperous Farmer

Several years ago as dean of a college, I visited a prosperous farmer whose son and daughter were students at my school. All the way to their parent's house, they spoke in the highest terms of their dad. I soon found out why.

After breakfast the first morning, I looked up and saw the father in the kitchen helping his wife with the dishes.

A little later I glanced through the window — he was out washing his son's car. During the day the daughter used her dad's car, while he used the truck. Finally, I asked him why.

"It's my way of saying a special thank you for the kids wanting to come back home. And I'm helping my wife so she has more time to spend with the kids."

This pattern continued the entire weekend. The mother and father slept on cots in the basement so the guests could have the best rooms in the house and the children could use their own rooms.

This man was no slave. He was not henpecked. He didn't undertake all those tasks every day, but he was willing to pitch in on special days. He was not spoiling his children. Nor was he ordered around or imposed upon.

His attitude was catching. The children helped him with the farm chores. They pitched in and helped with the housework.

Dad had set the tone. It was Jesus who said of Himself:

> For even the Son of Man did not come to be served, but to serve, and to give his life a ransom for many (Mark 10:45).

Jesus, Himself, said:

> . . .whoever wants to become great among you must be your servant (Mark 10:43).

> Give, and it will be given to you. A good measure, pressed down, shaken together and running over, will be poured into your lap. For with the measure you use, it will be measured to you (Luke 6:38).

Good will makes working out the details of life simple. When it doesn't exist, the activities you engage in are empty and unrewarding.

A Broken Example

For instance, a couple brought their teenage son to see me because he refused to go to church. This is his side of the story:

"Why should I go to church? Look at the way my parents treat each other. For instance, last Sunday morning we were sitting at the breakfast table, and my father refused to talk to mother.

"She, in turn, wouldn't even look at him. After breakfast, Dad turned to me and said:

'Get ready. You're going to church.'

"They forced me to go to church. All the way to church they didn't exchange a word. We pulled into the parking lot, and when we got out of the car, Dad offered Mom his arm. She took it.

"Between the parking lot and the church *you would have thought they were friends or something*!

"She cuddled up to him and smiled at him. They were friendly and congenial, and they acted that way all through church.

"Then, on the way home, they refused to talk to each other. Why should I go to church?"

My answer to him was:

"You got me. I wouldn't want to turn out like your father or mother either. I hate to say it, young man, but don't judge the church — or God — by the conduct of your parents." The best way to make church attendance attractive to the boy is for him to see his parents mellowing and easier to live with the older they get.

Your example is the key.

Dad, Pay Attention to Us!

Ralph has this viewpoint. "When I come home I figure my work is done. I'm home. And it's up to my wife and family to make me comfortable. After all, I'm the man of the house. I work all day and deserve a rest."

Ken feels more or less the same way. His son has a habit of harrassing him with an endless stream of questions as soon as he comes through the door. Ken has constructed a defense against this. He sets his son down beside him and starts reading the evening paper. His son talks on.

Ken gives out with an occasional :"Uh huh . . . No . . . Oh? . . . Yes . . ."

One evening this solid line of defense got him into trouble. On this night, he had ignored nearly all of the boy's questions, when he suddenly "came to" for one.

65

"What do you do all day down at your office?"

Upset over being pestered with unimportant questions, he tried to throw the boy's question aside by shooting out absent-mindedly:

"Oh . . .nothing."

After a thoughtful pause, the boy asked, "Dad, how do you know when you're through?"

Sometimes the child gets his revenge — and it's funny. What's not funny is Dad's approach to his children. What is he telling that little question machine beside him? Even though he has his son on the couch next to him, his mind is somewhere else. Children get the message — soon.

The Process

There are many similarities between running a business and running a family. In either organization the leader is fully responsible for the success of the organization. It is his task to see to it that plans, budgets, standards, and rules are set up. He must provide the supervision and training necessary to reach the objectives.

What a President Does

Permit me to share with you how this worked in my company and then make comparisons to the family. We started from scratch, and over a period of five years we built a chain of six restaurants involving 250 employees and several millions of dollars annually. Some of my duties as president were:

1. Set the objectives
2. Provide the finances
3. Provide buildings and equipment
4. Determine standards of quality and service
5. Set policies and rules
6. Provide standards of performance
7. Provide training and supervision
8. Provide maintenance of property and equipment
9. Provide cost controls
10. Delegate responsibility and authority

I didn't do this by myself. I set up the following

group of people to supervise the work: (1) one general manager (2) two assistants to the general manager (3) six managers (4) twelve assistant managers (5) one office manager.

The standards, policies, procedures, and rules were not conceived by me and then handed down to the employees. They were created and changed primarily by daily interaction between the general manager and the manager. How does a president get 250 people pulling together? It can be summarized best by reminding you of a Bible passage referred to in the last chapter:

> Then make my joy complete by being like-minded, having the same love, being one in spirit and purpose. Do nothing out of selfish ambition or vain conceit, but in humility consider others better than yourselves (Phil. 2:2,3).

Cooperation requires continuous, ongoing discussion, review, and change *among people of goodwill.* This was especially true of the relationship between my general manager and myself. What is in my mind and what I am committed to must be accepted in the general manager's mind, for he must implement my ideas with the managers and assistant managers. I need to know his mind, accept and help implement his ideas.

Look back at that verse again. Notice the two words: likemindedness and agreement. Those are good words — and attitudes that are keys to the success of any good business or family.

Setting Up the Family/

How does this apply to the family? If you think of parenthood as a small business, the leaders are the husband and wife.

They start small. Just two people. But the family grows gradually, just like a business. The duties are as follows:

1. Set the objectives
2. Provide the finances
3. Provide food and clothing
4. Provide buildings and equipment

5. Provide maintenance of property and equipment
6. Guide the children
7. Determine standards of quality and service
8. Set policies and rules
9. Provide standards of performance
10. Provide training and supervision
11. Provide cost controls
12. Delegate responsibility and authority

See how similar this is to running a business? None of this is possible without a foundation of good will, commitment, and cooperation. To put it in biblical terms:

Submit to one another out of reverence for Christ (Eph. 5:21).

To put it another way, it is the job of any couple to design a harness *both of them will wear.* This is not the same as the husband designing a harness for his wife to wear which is of his design only. This is a cooperative effort. Both wear the harness, and it's made up of the above responsibilities.

What resources do a couple have? Time, talent, ability, money. A family is a small business, so it requires personal involvement. There is a president and an executive vice-president. And that's it. Few families can afford or want a cook, a gardener, a maid, or a business manager.

The Officers

The husband is the president. His wife may be smarter than he or may be able to get more done, which is an asset, not a liability.

In my company, for example, we had an employee who knew more about food than anyone else. But he wasn't president because he was more knowledgeable about food. He was an employee who carried much responsibility and authority and made many decisions on his own.

Managing the Family

How does the husband go about managing the family? Since this book is focusing on parenthood, I'll just select the topic of guiding children as an example of how a husband fills his role of managing a family. The rest of the family responsibilities may be handled much the same way.

My wife and I were both committed to doing what was necessary to guide our children. I say *were* because our children are grown up and are now pursuing their own careers.

Picture the two of us having a meeting about child management. I am the president. The family is my responsibility.

My wife is the world's greatest expert on the subject of our children. She is also the executive vice-president.

We must set limits, provide supervision and training. How does a president proceed when he has the world's greatest expert on his hands? The answer seems obvious. He leans heavily on her expertise. One would be foolish to ignore such a person. Before you would contradict or overrule this person, you had better have a good reason.

This is exactly how we proceeded. I delegated the responsibility and authority for child guidance to my wife. Their feeding, clothing, education, social life, and duties were her responsibility. In other words, she told me how things were to be handled. This is not a copout on my part. It's simply drawing upon the best talent available.

We did not have Eva's way of handling the children and Henry's way of handling the children. We had a way that both of us were committed to. We had common guidelines, policies, limits. Eva was in charge whether I was home or not. We were of the same mind.

Even though she was in charge, there was no doubt who the president was. But Eva was the executive vice-president with all the authority to act as needed.

Just as in a business, policies, procedures, and limits kept changing. It required continuous, on-going conversation to keep up to date. Changing is not a matter of argument but of negotiation and cooperation. It is not Eva's changing or my changing.

Rather, *we* change to something we are both committed to, if change is necessary. When there is good will, commitment, and cooperation undergirding an organization, hangups seldom occur.

At our house, Eva was in charge.

United We Stand

Occasionally, one of our children used to come running out to me as I came home at night and say:

"Dad, can I go out tonight?"

I was in the driveway, not even in the house yet. I was in no position to answer that question, and the reason was that the person who had been in charge of this outfit all day long was in the house and I hadn't had a chance to find out what had been going on.

That woman in the house was my friend. We were on the same management team. She was the authority. And what's more, she was executive vice-president of the family.

Wouldn't I have been foolish to make decisions on behalf of my children without consulting her? In business, if I came to a branch office and met the manager first, I wouldn't give him an opinion on any big decision until I had first talked to the general manager, now would I?

The same with my children. I couldn't give them an answer when I first came home. To put it in the business vernacular, I didn't have any data.

If you make a decision without data, you make a decision that may get you into trouble. It's a guess. And what's even more important, if a husband makes a decision without data, then he'd better be ready to change it immediately.

A Business Meeting at Home

In my regular business I have many meetings with the key man in the business. We sit down together and plan what is best for the future and evaluate what we've been doing in the past. We may make some changes. We may revise what we have been doing up to now.

It should be the same in a home. Marriage partners sit down and review the day, the week, or the interim while the husband has been away — or while the wife has been away.

70

You don't need to ask if there have been any problems while one of you has been gone. There'll be problems. The two basic questions are:

(1) What problems did you have you were able to solve? (2) What problems did you have you were unable to solve?

Then go from there.

Maybe you'll make some changes. The two of you may reevaluate the rules. Whatever, the job is to chart the course for your family.

Not two courses. One. Not one way when Dad is home and another way when Mom is home. I have heard children say:

"I can get along O.K. with my dad when he is home and Mom is gone." Or, "I can get along all right with my mother when she is home and Father is gone, but when they are together it is difficult because my parents do not agree."

Agreement and unity comprise the foundation on which you build an effective family life.

If you and your wife function as president and executive vice-president, you will discover that being in business for yourself — the family business — can be a lot of fun.

6 / Mom — Mrs. Executive Vice-President

6 / Mom — Mrs. Executive Vice- President

Some Kind of Woman!/

> A good wife who can find? She is far more precious than jewels (Prov. 31:10).

Proverbs 31 is an incredible chapter. Or, rather, it contains an incredible list of characteristics, roles, and responsibilities. And they are all found in the same woman! Here is that list:

Seamstress extraordinary
Small businesswoman
Purchaser of goods
Obtainer of food
Time and schedule organizer
Real estate purchaser
Physical fitness expert
Teacher
Ambitious
Fears the Lord
Clothes purchaser
Community worker
Good citizen
Social worker
Dietitian
Good dresser
Saleswoman

Tireless worker
Lets her job speak for itself
Praised by family and community alike

That's some kind of woman! Hardly someone who just keeps house.

Isn't it a pity we so often ignore the Bible? The roles and characteristics of the woman described in this chapter could serve as an outline for any woman's awareness course.

Yet modern-day literature would have us believe that the tremendous talent and ability residing in women is a recent discovery.

Any man who hasn't taken note of the fact that women are on a par with men as intelligent, creative people just hasn't been paying attention.

A Good Lesson

During my junior high school days, the local newspaper had a young writers' club. Our English teacher required all of us to write a weekly story for the club. She would pick the best story and send it to the paper for publication.

Nine out of ten weeks, the best story was written by one of the girls.

Also, during those days I was given charge of managing schoolwide candy sales to raise money for our extracurricular activities.

The two top "salesmen" were always girls.

I had another responsibility during my high school days that showed me something about women. I was assigned to be in charge of the mimeographing at the school. I started recruiting workers . . . some boys and some girls.

Of the two groups, I soon found that the girls proved more efficient, trustworthy, and cooperative than the boys.

In college, the top student in my class was a girl — dadgum her!

No matter what the rest of us did, she was always out there in front of us. Even so, being top student in the class wasn't enough for her. She also was president of several of the leading clubs at the school.

As I've made my way through the educational, business, and church worlds, I've noticed that a woman can run a vacation Bible school just as well, if not better, than a man. And in my business, the person we assigned to be in charge of the money was a woman.

I never cease to marvel at the skill and ease with which my wife can produce a delicious meal. The finest chef may match her skill, but I doubt if anyone could exceed her.

To her, cooking is fun.

People often visit us for the express purpose of seeing me. They might spend eight hours with me and only a half an hour with Eva (at a meal).

Even though I helped them, it seems that whenever they write back, what they remember most is Eva and her cooking — not me. Her outlook toward cooking shows.

It's also remarkable how quickly she can breeze through the house to straighten it up. And she takes care of our travel arrangements as competently as the finest travel agent.

The Constant Complaint

On the other hand, Janie, age forty-four, wails:

"There must be more meaning to life than this! In the morning, Dad and the kids all descend upon the kitchen, where I feed them breakfast.

"At noon, part of that original crew returns to have their stomachs filled again.

"Then they all disappear and I don't see them again until early evening when they suddenly materialize just in time to have their tummies filled again. Why, all our kitchen is . . . is a filling station!

"And I'm the attendant."

Mary Ann, age twenty-eight, echoes the sentiments:

"All through high school, my parents saved money for my college. I worked after school and during summers. Then, together we struggled to pay my way through college. Finally, I got my degree.

"Then, after I got out of college, instead of using that degree, I got married. Now, I change diapers, sweep the floor, cook meals, and wash dishes all day. Did I need a college degree for that? I've never felt so worthless in all my life."

There is a lot of difference between grinding out breakfast like a station attendant and providing nutritious meals and fun for the family and their guests.

Janie and Mary Ann ought to sit down and talk with their husbands and solve a real problem in their family management.

Women are not alone, though.

Nose Holes and Soggy Mouths

Ralph, who works in a kitchen cabinet shop, sees himself as a craftsman — a maker of wooden works of art.

Another employee in the same shop has a different outlook. He is a grumpy, crabby griper who only saws boards, inhales sawdust, and gets glue all over his fingers.

Both do the same job. Both make beautiful cabinets.

Details can be wearisome, can't they? Have you ever thought of how many ear holes and nose holes a doctor examines each day? Does he think of his job in terms of nose holes or in terms of healing people?

What about the soggy mouths a dentist looks into during his working hours? Does he look at it as a job examining soggy mouths or a job of helping people to good dental health?

Mr. Everything

Let's take a look at a unique situation: Valerie has a business of her own and her husband, Erik, stays at home and does the housework. He sees the children off to school each day. He helps with the shopping and the cooking, but this still leaves lots of time on his hands.

He's become a volunteer worker at church — and a busy one. He's perfectly happy and loves his role.

To meet Erik, you'd think you had met the ideal

man. Big. Handsome. Personable.

But he is a loafer.

He once had a responsible job. Then came a demotion, and then another. Finally, he was fired — but for laziness.

So Valerie, a competent, responsible person, stepped into the gap. She got a job, and then started her own business. For ten years, she has supported the family.

Valerie's situation is exactly what many wives long for. She is free from the routines of managing a home.

But all is not well. She prefers to be a homemaker.

"It's not fair, Dr. Brandt," says she. "I want to be home doing housework and taking care of the kids. Erik won't let me."

There it is — according to my observations in the consulting room — the basic cause of marital discord: *conflict and ill will between couples.*

The routines must be handled, no doubt about that. The debate is over who does what.

For Erik and Valerie, it's a standoff. It's been a ten-year debate. No one has the last word, so the issue can't be settled.

Any woman — or man — needs to be effectively and happily busy. But contentment doesn't come by dropping one set of routines for another. Erik and Valerie found that out.

The division of responsibilities between a husband and wife is, of course, negotiable. A couple can only come to mutually agreeable decisions as both parties are committed to the mutual interests of one another and final authority is established.

The Swimming Instructor

Sarah was not effectively busy. She had four children — ages 2 through 14 — and a husband who was in business for himself.

"I don't have any big trouble with the children. I host the parties for Edgar when he's entertaining. I take care of the house. I help out in the business. Still, I've got a lot of time on my hands — time that I don't want to spend vegetating in front of *The Edge of Night.*"

79

So she and her husband decided that she should volunteer to teach a swimming class at the YMCA. It wasn't that she didn't like housework or managing children. She had time on her hands — and a busy mind.

Her husband wholeheartedly encouraged Sarah. And the baby-sitting service at the YMCA enabled her to take the baby with her to her class.

Sarah was good — so good, that within a year she was teaching four courses at the YMCA. Even though she was now spending a total of about ten hours on four different days at the Y, she still easily managed to meet her primary responsibilities as mother and wife.

She took on more. She enrolled in a scuba course and passed it with ease. After two years of service, she had added scuba teaching to her list of courses. Already her students included little children and high schoolers.

Another year later, she was in charge of the lifesaving classes and had been chosen to head up the new scuba club.

So it went. A year later, Sarah was named "Volunteer of the Year." When the aquatic director moved to another YMCA, the board asked Sarah to replace him.

By now, Sarah's involvement had become a family affair. Two of her children had joined the swim team. Her second oldest son had a job at the YMCA. The youngest was starting to take swimming classes, too.

Sarah refined her approach to the job of aquatic director. By the end of her first year, she had done such a good job that she was asked by the board to join the staff full-time.

And only five years after she had gone to "teach a swimming course at the Y."

There were occasional tensions in the family, but they were few. Edgar was totally behind her successful efforts at the YMCA.

However, he had one consistent but quiet disagreement. He didn't approve of her scuba diving under ice in the winter. At first she pooh-poohed his doubts:

"It's the most beautiful time to dive. The water is entirely clear. On sunny days, the scene is incredible."

Edgar didn't insist she quit, but he did not drop his occasional quiet disagreement. She realized he was greatly concerned with her ice diving. It was one of those things she felt was up for negotiation in a marriage. So she quit.

A sobering sidelight. Shortly after she quit ice diving, the scuba club lost one of its divers on such a dive.

Today, Sarah is one of the most outstanding YMCA aquatic directors in the Midwest. Under her leadership, her swimming teams have won six straight state championships and even occasional national championships.

She also is making very good money, which is helping put the two oldest children through college.

Sarah could have become bored. But, while balancing her primary goals beautifully, she went out and became effectively busy.

The Girl Who Was Tops in Her Class

The same was true of Linda. A very creative person, she had graduated from college at the top of her class and then immediately married.

She eventually had two children, but it just wasn't enough. She was becoming bored. She suggested to her husband they start a children's program for their small church, which had trouble recruiting leaders.

"But I want to do a good job," she said when she suggested it to him.

"I'm all for it. Let's go," he replied.

Together, they threw themselves into the task and came up with a unique program for the children of their church who ranged in age from 3 to 12.

Drawing on her training, she suggested a program that had from fifteen to thirty time slots, ranging from as short as ten seconds to never longer than three minutes. She helped plan the weekly schedule. She contacted speakers, picked up films and film strips. She did artwork, set up puppet ideas, and started a Christian books reading program. The program helped turn the entire trend of the church around. Before it had been losing families with elementary age children. Now, they stayed. The church

81

grew. Others heard about the program and wanted to know more. The church was so delighted that on Linda's birthday they sent her a beautiful bouquet of flowers with the signature:

"Happy birthday! From the parents of Grace Church."

Linda and her husband were asked to write articles about the basic concepts of their approach.

Also, the two of them decided Linda was the better storyteller of the team. So she has been telling a series of stories for the weekly gatherings. Now, she is working on the project of making some of the stories into books.

And it wouldn't have happened if Linda and her husband hadn't realized she wasn't effectively busy.

Two Volunteers

Marilyn is also a volunteer. She spends one night a week at an international airport serving as a volunteer for traveler's aid.

She just bubbles over with all sorts of rewarding stories. One was about the time she helped a man find a hotel even though he couldn't speak a word of English.

Then there was the man she took downtown to a bank and helped him to learn how to make change in American money.

Or the time one scared traveler arrived only to find her expected friend wasn't there to meet her. Marilyn took over. She found out who she was expecting, got in touch with the missing greeter, and made the traveler happy and comfortable during the wait.

She loves her volunteer work.

Then, there's Margie.

She is a bitter, resentful, a woman who constantly gripes — about her home and about her husband.

She, too, is a volunteer worker . . . with the Red Cross. She's a driver.

A person needs to go downtown to get a welfare check. Or someone gives some blood and then passes out. An elderly person needs to go to the hospital for vital shots.

Margie drives them — a very useful type of volunteer work.

But she doesn't enjoy it — not one bit. She gripes about the "miserable people." She gripes just as much as she does about her home and husband.

Two volunteers . . . Marilyn and Margie. Why are they so different? They have two different problems. Marilyn needs to be effectively busy. Margie needs to experience a new relationship with Jesus Christ.

Busyness doesn't take care of your spirit. You must make a distinction between dealing with your spirit and dealing with untapped use of your talent and intelligence.

Two Professors /

When I was going to college, I met a professor who was the main influence on my views of parenthood. Her name was Ethel Waring, and she was an incredible person.

She was happy. She was radiant. She was an inspiring college professor. What made her that way? Simple. She was a happy woman.

I know another woman college professor. But her reason for teaching is not so she will be effectively busy. She is teaching to get away from her husband, whom she hates.

Her college teaching hasn't made a happy woman out of her, because it's an escape from another situation that she refuses to solve.

Her busyness has made her even more unhappy, for she keeps comparing her husband (who is really a nice, competent guy) with some of the other male professors. She goes home and often takes potshots at her husband.

What is she doing? Multiplying her misery by not only being a hateful woman toward her husband but also being a phony at work.

Good-bye to Scrambled Eggs /

Statistics tell a story, too. More than any time in history, women who can't face the scrambled eggs in the morning are becoming working mothers.

More than sixty percent of all women with children age 6 to 17 worked last year. The number one reason given was economic necessity. Right behind that reason, however, was boredom. It's obvious there is widespread discontentment among women — and men.

For a decade I've been employing people . . . men and women. Getting a job does not make a man or a woman happy. Employ an unhappy person, and you have to work with an unhappy person. The source of happiness lies outside yourself.

> But the fruit of the Spirit is love, joy, peace, patience, kindness, goodness, faithfulness, gentleness and self-control. Against such things there is no law (Gal. 5:22, 23).

Competence and intelligence . . . organizational ability. These are characteristics of both men and women. They need to be expressed.

But this expression does not change the spirit, whether it's a man or a woman. There are men who are wasting their talents, too.

Meet the Veep

In most businesses, the two top officers are the president and the executive vice-president. The president oversees the company and helps set the main policies, the main plan, for the company. He may travel many different places to represent the company.

But when it comes to the day-in-and-day-out running of the business, the executive vice-president is usually the key officer, for it is the executive vice-president who really sees that things keep going.

While the president may be responsible for many final decisions, he rarely makes a decision without leaning heavily on the advice of someone in the company, usually the executive V.P., who is a very knowledgeable, authoritative person in his own right. These men are friends and sense a high degree of accomplishment as they work together. It is difficult to distinguish one's input from the other.

This is a perfect description of the roles of a father and a mother. While dad might be known as the head of the home and responsible for many of the ultimate decisions, he doesn't run the family on a day-in-and-day-out basis. The mother does that. She is the executive vice-president.

If she does her homework, she is the most knowledgeable, best-informed person in the organization. As the years go by and she grows in her knowledge of the children, her input becomes increasingly valuable. As her recommendations are put into practice, the resulting success makes her an increasingly valuable person in the organization. Her influence is enormous and her wisdom is one of the most important assets of the organization.

Such an authoritative person (an expert) makes decisions as necessary within the policies of the organization without consulting anyone. Managing the family is a responsibility many women can handle easily with much time to spare.

Expanding Mom's Role

There are some mothers who couldn't possibly take on any additional family responsibilities. Then, there are those moms who breeze through the chores at home and are ready for something else by 10 o'clock every morning. My wife is that way.

When my wife and I first started in this business of raising a family, we got together and listed all of our responsibilities. (Notice I said *our* responsibilities, not *my wife's* responsibilities or *my* responsibilities.)

Just a few of the many we detailed were: housecleaning, money management, cooking, writing, radio work, children, cleaning the yard, travel agent, running a business, raising money, food purchasing.

Then we divvied them up — Eva got money management, travel agent, housecleaning, cooking, children, food purchasing and a bunch more. I was assigned writing, radio work, cleaning the yard, running a business, raising money. These were assignments on the basis of training, ability, interest, and necessity.

How we met the responsibilities was not the question. The assignment was simple: these were the responsibilities each of us was to carry out.

If my wife decided to add responsibilities outside the home . . . fine. But she would have to figure out some way to carry out her primary tasks.

The same went for any other activities I took on. It

85

was O.K. as long as I kept the primary activities going. Of course, they kept changing as the children grew and demands on our time changed.

In all our planning and assigning, we kept one thing in mind — that plan of ours had to be a family plan. We made sure to remember that it was a Brandt plan, not Henry's plan or Eva's plan. It was our plan, and we had to carry out our responsibilities.

If you're not effectively busy at home, the next time you have one of those business meetings between husband and wife, well, volunteer for some more work!

It sure beats being bored.

Dirty Uniforms or Bad Service?

Many decisions can and should be made without involving the president of a company or the husband in a family.

A meeting is being held in a business. Present are the general manager (number two man in the organization), his two assistants, and six managers. The question under discussion: a letdown in five of the restaurants on uniform cleanliness and crispness.

"I'll admit it," says one of the managers. "We have let down on this, but only because of the policy."

"Right," says another manager. "If we follow the policy and send an employee home every time she reports to work with a uniform that isn't neat, then she gets mad and threatens to quit."

"And business is booming so much, that if we are short even one waitress because of such a policy it really cuts into our ability to give the people good service."

"No good service . . . no good business," adds another.

"I disagree," exclaims one of the assistants. "We've always held to a standard of cleanliness, right?"

Everyone agrees.

"Well, if we start allowing our uniforms to get sloppy, the entire operation begins to get sloppy. Let down a standard here and then a standard there. Pretty soon, we're sloppy all around. And then we'll really lose customers."

86

The debate is now on. And after a little more discussion, it is obvious the group is hopelessly split. It is time for the general manager to make a decision. The neat uniform policy will stand. Everyone accepts it and that's that.

After the meeting is over, the general manager calls me up and gives me a verbal report. That's the end of it. The authority for the general manager to operate this way comes from the president. It is based on the general manager's record. He has first hand contact with the managers and on the basis of his performance has demonstrated his competence.

"I've Made Some Changes Around Here!"

A family organization is much smaller than a restaurant chain, of course. There is a president and executive vice-president, or man and wife.

Joe and Marie are sitting at the kitchen table. Two boys, ages eight and ten, are playing outside.

Marie: I made some changes around here.

Joe: What are they?

Marie: I've pushed bedtime up a half hour and now the kids must take their shoes off on the landing.

Joe: O.K.

That night, Joe puts the children to bed. This was Marie's job, but she was too tired and asked him to do it. Each boy griped to dad because he had to take his shoes off on the landing. His response to them was:

"That's the way it is."

Go, Team, Go!

The authority for Marie to operate this way comes from Joe. It is based on her record. She has firsthand contact on a daily basis with the children and on the basis of her performance has demonstrated her competence.

Guiding children is the responsibility of the organization. Joe and Marie are a team. They work together. They care about each other. Of course he will put the children to bed if she is tired. In their style of life, he may put them to bed often. The pattern of responsibilities is a negotiable matter. There is no competition here, just cooperation.

What else does Marie do besides keep house and manage the children? Whatever she and Joe agree is reasonable.

What else does Joe do besides his income-producing job? Whatever he and Marie agree is reasonable.

Agreement is the key word. It's a team effort. Unresolved conflicts are the soil for sick marriages.

Nancy Wanted a Washing Machine . . .

Nancy and Kevin could not agree on who should control the money, and there were other conflicts of opinion. There were many verbal barrages. She wanted a washer and dryer. He said she would get them only over his dead body. Her response was to go buy them.

In retaliation, Kevin went on a drinking spree that lasted several days. For spite, he bought a new station wagon. Nancy did not enjoy her appliances. They were a rebuke to her every time she used them. Nor did her husband enjoy driving that new station wagon.

Here were two people who had acquired some equipment that should have given them joy and satisfaction. Instead, these useful things became a continuing bone of contention. Behind the strife over money was the unsettled question of submission. Both persons were asserting a spirit of independence and selfishness.

They were hardly a team.

Two Voices – One Tune

Once my daughter came to me and said:

"The church youth group is going roller skating. And Mom said I can't go. Can I go?"

I wasn't in a position to make that decision. I didn't know if my wife had said that. So I simply checked with my wife, who replied:

"Well, the condition for going roller skating was that she have her homework done."

"That's right," I added, "we agreed on that."

"Well, she doesn't have it done."

That was simple; case dismissed. However, this is what happened in another family. Carole had asked her mother if she might go roller skating with the church group and Mom replied:

"No, you were at prayer meeting last night, and you studied late the night before."

"Ah, let her go," Dad cut in. "She's only young once."

"But Carole needs her rest," Mom insisted. Then the seesaw argument began, and both mother and father were soon angry.

The incident was a common one in Carole's life. As a result her head and heart spun with confusion and revolt so much that she eventually came to me for help.

This is deadly. Frequently the husband has one plan and the wife another. When the husband goes away to work, the wife says to herself:

"Finally . . . he's gone! Now we can get back to normal around here."

It's so important that parents speak with two voices but only one tune. That's the way Joe and Marie decided to do it.

Call of the Beauty Shop

Joe and Marie agreed to go camping. But finding a time proved difficult. Joe wanted to go this weekend, but Marie had a beauty shop appointment Saturday afternoon.

After some discussion about cancelling, Joe realized it would be an unnecessary nuisance for her. He couldn't go the following week, so they planned camping in three weeks.

This is no big deal among friends who really care about each other.

When they did go, they were all together on the project. At the camp site, Marie became acquainted with the lady in the tent next door. Marie was enjoying frying hamburgers beside the lake, while her neighbor was griping about being dragged away from home to endure the nuisance of outdoor cooking.

They were in the same spot with similar equip-

89

ment, both cooking beside a lake. The difference was in the spirit of the women and their relationships with their husbands.

Now . . . the Children

We're through talking about the man now. And we're through talking about the woman. We're assuming a contented man and a contented woman. So let's get on with the job of parenthood.

Each family should have as its goal:

> Train up a child in the way he should go, and when he is old he will not depart from it (Prov. 22:6).

This is not a woman's job — nor a man's. It is the task of the partnership. Assuming good will, friendship, and commitment, two highly competent people will get on with the job.

If you were to sum up the content of the last chapter and this one in one word, that word would be "submission." Assuming good will, we mean a man and a woman submitting to a mutually acceptable and agreeable plan for guiding the affairs of the family. It is like wearing a two-part harness.

When a decision is to be made, and the facts involved lead a couple to a stalemate, the husband will settle it — after careful consideration of his wife's recommendations. He should have some very good reasons if he overrules her judgment. Put into biblical terms:

> Submit to one another out of reverence for Christ. Wives, submit to your husbands as to the Lord. For the husband is the head of the wife as Christ is the head of the church, his body, of which he is the Savior. Now as the church submits to Christ, so also wives should submit to their husbands in everything. Husbands, love your wives, just as Christ loved the church and gave himself up for her to make her holy, cleansing her by the washing with water through the word, and to present her to himself as a radiant church, without stain or wrinkle or any other blemish, but holy and blameless. In this same way, husbands ought to love their wives as their own bodies. He who loves his wife loves himself (Eph. 5:21-28).

What a partnership must do to guide the children is the subject of the rest of this book.

III / Discipline That Counts

7 / The Freedom
of Boundaries

7 / The Freedom of Boundaries

The Perfect Play

There is a football stadium in my state which holds 100,000 people. Every fall it's filled repeatedly by people who fight traffic jams, are jostled by crushing crowds, suffer through rainstorms, mud, sleet and snow for several hours.

What is it that provides the magnet for drawing these people into this stadium? What causes millions of other fans to gather around their television sets at the same time? There's just one reason.

It is the pleasure and satisfaction that comes from watching eleven men cooperate as one unit to produce in a sudden, dramatic moment — a long run, a beautiful pass — a touchdown!

I've been in the University of Michigan stadium when everyone leaped to his feet at the same time and cheered.

What could possibly happen that would cause 100,000 people to do the same thing at the same time?

It's the perfect play.

To pull off the perfect play, a player must be willing to subject his own will to a common cause. And when it's done right, the perfect play is a beautiful, magical thing to watch.

What makes the perfect play possible is everyone subjecting himself to one plan and everyone working together whether it was his idea or not.

Each man has his job and can use any legal technique he desires. Every man doing his job . . . and with flair. That's what creates the perfect play. That's what is beautiful to watch.

Notice. Flair isn't enough. Every man doing his own thing with flair doesn't make it. Everyone has to be working together.

Refereeing

In a football game, the home and visiting teams — even the hometown and visiting fans — all go by the same rules and boundaries. These rules are published in a book. You can't understand the game if you don't know the rules. In this book we will use the word "limits" to mean rules and boundaries.

Making sure the players stay within the limits is the job of the officials. If a player breaks a limit, the referee penalizes the team. He and his team have to take the consequences.

That's no big deal. You just take your consequences and the game goes on. You protest too much, and you get kicked out of the game — with the approval of the crowd.

The referee's interpretation of the limits is final, if not perfect. That's why, if you argue, you get kicked out of the game. Not off the team. Out of the game.

If two opponents get into a fist fight, the referee stops it immediately (with the possible exception of hockey). That's all there is to it. It's not limits that stop the game. They make the game.

Your Limits Make You Unique

The word "football" tells you many things. It settles the shape of the ball, the dimensions of the playing field, the rules of the game, even the clothes you wear.

The word "family" also tells you many things. Your limits make you unique. If we use a name, say the Landrum family, it tells you many things about the choices that family made about how things should go.

It's up to Mr. and Mrs. Landrum to make those choices. When they do, the word Landrum will mean something to them as a family. Translated into a list, it would look something like this:

your address	television time
type of house	how you dress
your church	how you handle your clothes
your school	house rules
style of recreation	choice of toys
bedtime	use of toys
meal time	neatness
table manners	contact with friends

entertaining at home

This is not meant to be a complete list. At a glance it is easy to see what is involved in setting up limits. If you have one set for him and another for her, you put your children into two games rather than one.

In football, all coaches, referees, and players everywhere go by the same limits. In a family, both parents go by the same limits. Remember, your limits make your family unique. Consider Philippians 2:2, 3:

> Then make my joy complete by being like-minded, having the same love, being one in spirit and purpose. Do nothing out of selfish ambition or vain conceit, but in humility consider others better than yourselves.

"Of one mind . . . ?" Right.

Like . . . at bedtime.

You've got three children. The preschooler goes to bed at 7:30. The grade schooler at 8:30. The junior high child at 10:00.

Now, there is much creativity possible in order to get them to bed.

But at night, bedtime is bedtime. And not "oh, just-this-one-more-TV-program" time. There's no question about when the child goes to bed. It doesn't matter if it's Mom or Dad doing the job.

What approach do you take to make sure the limits are kept? That's up to you. Do it however you want. But do it.

97

Remember the magnet that draws people into the football stadium. It's the thrill and satisfaction of watching eleven men cooperate to produce a sudden, dramatic run, a beautiful pass, or the perfect touchdown play.

Parenthood is like that. Its fascination comes in working together to pull off a pleasant meal, an evening marked by the cheery laughter of happy children, getting all three of them to bed smoothly, easily, happily.

It doesn't happen very often, but you keep trying, cooperating, working together — within the limits you are both committed to.

A Miracle?

There is a day-to-day variation of how much energy it takes for you to do your job. To accept responsibility for getting the children to bed is half the battle. Usually, the preschooler is the first barrier. But not tonight. This time, it's different for a change.

You just scoop him up and put him to bed. Phew, that was easy for once.

The grade school child provides more of a challenge. She varies from night to night. Some nights, she goes to bed at your first suggestion. Other nights, she's so worn out, she just disappears. Then another evening might find her full of vim and vigor and nowhere near ready to go to bed.

Tonight, she just disappears.

Two down and one to go.

Usually your junior higher resists bedtime. So it takes more creativity to help her meet her limit. Some nights she would be willing to discuss the merits of going to bed — or anything — for an hour. Just to avoid going to bed.

But tonight — no problem.

You did it.

The perfect play.

Those Vim and Vigor Nights

On those vim and vigor nights, you might want to set up a rough race around the block, giving the smallest children big head starts.

Or maybe a relaxing bath is the best thing. Possibly you may want to calm your child down by reading him a book. Do whatever is necessary.

"Oh . . . no!" you say. "That's too much work." Well, a healthy, busy child will create more work for you on those active nights. You want a busy, healthy child. Still, bedtime is bedtime.

On such nights, don't expect the perfect plays. Just figure on a little more time and effort that both husband and wife will have to put forth.

Your willingness to stick to bedtime might be creating challenges for you. Your teenager is alert, full of vim and vigor. Good student, busy. One of the reasons might be that she gets enough sleep. She's well-rested. Your own good administration makes getting a teenager to bed on time a creative effort.

The task varies from night to night, but the limits stay the same.

Children Are People Too!

What about their attitudes? Won't limits ruin them emotionally? We are talking about guiding children, not changing their spirit. They get their joy from God — just as you do.

They are people, just like you. Remember what people are like:

> For what I do is not the good I want to do; no, the evil I do not want to do — this I keep on doing (Rom. 7:19).

> All we like sheep have gone astray; we have turned every one to his own way (Isa. 53:6).

Your children need a Savior, too. They have the same drives we do. That's why their Christian education is important. That's why it's a twenty-year job.

Limits Provide Security

I didn't think too much about it the evening my daughter approached me just as I was ready to walk up on the platform:

"Hey, Dad, could I have the keys to the car? After

the meeting, I want to take a carload of kids up to Santa Cruz."

"O.K.," I said, without thinking.

Then I went to the platform to make my speech about how important it is for a man and his wife to be agreed on limits and be committed to them. After I finished I went to a large foyer in the back of the auditorium. There were hundreds of people milling around back there.

My daughter came up with her carload of friends behind her and said:

"Dad, I want the keys now."

My wife was standing there and she said, "I told you you couldn't go."

Well, there were some people standing around who heard us. They started assembling another little congregation there to see how the speaker would handle this.

You can't think of everything, especially when you are traveling. But we had a limit at our house that said the first parent you ask, that's it. All I had to do was to find out whom she had asked first. It turned out she had asked her mother first.

This is what you call "testing the limits." You can expect your children to pick times like that to do it. You see, I had to make a decision quickly. Will we raise children or save face? We were committed to raising children. So I said to my daughter:

"You know the answer. You asked your mother first."

Her response was: "But Dad, you are embarrassing me in front of all these people."

Now this is a child putting pressure on you, isn't it? I am embarrassing her in front of all these people. I want to point out that for her not to get the car when she knew perfectly well what the limit was, and for us to hold to the limit, is security — dependability. This is refereeing.

It is crucial and important that your children realize their mother and father set limits and can be depended on to carry them out.

Commitment or Confusion . . .

I listened to a story in the consulting room that points up the need for commitment to the family plan.

The parents brought their boy to see me because he was smoking and couldn't be trusted. The parents were concerned about it, and they made a deal with him.

"If you promise to quit smoking, we will buy you a bicycle." "It's a deal."

So they bought him a bicycle, but it wasn't long before they realized he was smoking again.

"If you will quit smoking," they said, "we will send you to your favorite summer camp."

"It's a deal" — again without hesitation. But when he came home from summer camp they discovered he was smoking again. Finally, at this point, they brought him to me because they were concerned they had a son who wouldn't keep his word. They couldn't trust him.

I had a talk with the boy and this is what I found out. His father had an idea that you shouldn't have ice cream during the day. Do you know what this boy's mother would do? Every once in awhile she would pick the kids up from school, and they would stop in to get an ice cream sundae. The only stipulation was — *don't tell Dad.*

Nice lady!

There was something else the boy told me. These people went to a church where one of the standards you accepted when you joined the church was that you would not drink alcoholic beverages. Now Dad liked a good cold beer when he came home from work, but he got everyone to promise that "mum's the word" when it came to his beer.

Where did this young fellow get the idea of making an agreement and then breaking it? Isn't it obvious he observed it from his mother? And also from his father?

These people pretended they were accepting some limits and then went ahead and broke them. Why shouldn't the boy make a deal with Dad and not intend to keep it?

These parents were teaching by example.

The Game /

So, now it's time to set limits for the family. Think of it. The two people in all the world who care the most about your children — you and your wife — are planning the finest possible life for them.

Doesn't that sound great?

What could be more fun than two parents deciding what is best for the children?

Setting limits doesn't deal with the problem of human nature, the sinfulness of your children. Limits don't change children's attitudes, or their spirit.

By setting limits, (1) you allow your children some freedom of choice, (2) you make things a little more predictable, and (3) you provide a framework for dealing with your children.

Definition of Freedom /

And there is the possibility that no matter how reasonable a limit is in your judgment, your children will not agree that it provides them with reasonable freedom. Remember, you are the leaders, not your children.

What is freedom? I like this definition: Freedom is the length of a leash from a chosen stake. Picture that. The leash can be short or long. It can be adjusted. There is a lot of freedom between the stake and the outer boundary. When it comes to children you can give them more or less freedom, depending on how they handle it. Freedom can be adjusted.

I once was driving on a highway in Texas, and my companion said to me: "You are now on the biggest ranch in the entire world." It was so big that the highway we were on was running *through* the ranch, like a big driveway. Along the road were fences to keep livestock in. There were many cows behind those fences — and they had incredible freedom.

Why you couldn't even see the other fences that kept them on this ranch. The fences were so far away they were over the horizon.

Some kind of freedom!

And yet, wouldn't you know, there was one cow straining her neck through the fence to get a blade of grass on the other side.

102

The cow had acres to choose from. Yet it opted for an unattainable space covering just a few inches.

I thought: how much like people. No matter how broad the limits are, your children will test some of them. When the testing time comes, it's hard for a child to see how limits provide any freedom.

Limits: a Field to Play On

In our family, we looked at limits as areas of freedom . . . of choice of activities. For example: We had designated certain areas for play. In the living room, you could read or play the record player.

In the family room, you could play with blocks, push-pull toys . . . games . . . an easel. And the only limitation was: put the game or toy back when you get through.

There were even some things you could do in the kitchen. You could always help with the dishes. You could help scrape a carrot, peel potatoes, pick the holes clean in the colander with a toothpick. Mom made all these tasks fun. Or you could sit at the table and talk to her.

Then there was the basement. You had many choices down there — a swing . . . screwed into the rafters — a tricycle and a wagon.

The real attraction was a piano box, which, on one day would serve as a skyscraper, the next day as a submarine, the following day a house. You could make anything out of it you wanted.

There was a bench, with a hammer and nails, and a saw. Wood was cut to size so you could nail pieces together.

Outside, there was a swing set, which had a swing, parallel bars, rings. There was another wagon. And a sandbox . . . full of toys.

In all these activity areas, the only limitations were that you (1) didn't throw things or (2) hit anyone.

And you could make all the noise you wanted in these areas except for the living room and the family room. These were conversation rooms.

The limits defined the options.

103

Make Life . . . a Little More Predictable

Earlier we referred to the Landrum family. The limits they set for the family are part of their uniqueness. Let's examine some:

> *Eat a balanced meal.*
> *Don't eat crackers or other such foods on the living room couch.*
> *Pick up your toys when you're through with them.*
> *Hang up your clothes in the closet.*
> *The family sits together at church.*
> *Each child has a regular bedtime.*

Do these sound reasonable? There are many more you could add to your list. Some you'd disagree with and eliminate. That's OK. What's important is that you and your partner agree on the limits.

When you set the limits:

1. Make them reachable and reasonable according to your judgment.

2. Make as few as possible.

Remember, limits give you a basis for dealing with your children. If you are consistent, then it helps your children *to know what to expect from you.* But limits don't transform children into obedient people.

A Framework for Dealing With Your Child

Tony discovered this after going out of his way to set what he thought was a reasonable limit with his eleven-year-old son. He even got his son to participate in making the decision.

"Let's set a reasonable limit, son."

Before supper, you wash your hands.

His son agreed. "Yes, Dad, that's reasonable."

Until just before supper. Then he suddenly disagreed with Tony. After all, his hands weren't that dirty, and he was hungry and ready for supper.

Tony had to march an unhappy child to the sink and make him wash his hands.

"Did You Make Your Bed?"

Let's take a look at one limit my wife and I agreed was reasonable and would apply to all our children. It was:

Before you come down for breakfast, make your bed.

We had no problem with the girls. It was a different story with our son. Every morning, you would hear the same conversation, just as my son bounced down the stairs:

"Son, did you make your bed?"

"No."

"Well, then, go back up and make it."

How often do you have to tell a child to make his bed before he does it automatically?

Would you believe twenty years?

Twenty years? Sounds like something went wrong. What was wrong with our formula? After all, it was a reasonable limit. Also, it was well within my son's abilities to do it.

Still . . . every morning we would have to get involved. Most of the time (nearly every day) he needed a reminder. Occasionally he needed more than a reminder. He needed some assistance up the stairs.

He was waiting for that day when we wouldn't remind or assist. Occasionally, that would happen. That was a flaw in our administration. Usually, we did remind or help him.

See? Reasonable limits don't necessarily make obedient children. How long did this go on? Twenty years.

Oh, there were occasional shockers. One time he made his bed without reminders every day for a week.

I could hardly believe it.

"We've finally done it," I congratulated my wife.

But we hadn't. He'd done it right for seven days. Then he missed a day . . . then he missed the next 364 . . . or was it 730?

That didn't make us angry — usually. When it did, my spirit was the problem, not his behavior. To correct my spirit meant confessing *my* sin (anger) to God, be forgiven, and cleansed. At that moment, I need to practice step 4 as mentioned on page 44 earlier in this book.

Summing Up

To sum up this matter of limits: I. They should provide freedom. 2. They should make life more predictable. 3. They should provide a framework for dealing with your children.

Limits should have the following characteristics:

☆ They should help a child foresee what is going to happen and what is expected of him.

☆ They should be reachable, reasonable, and clearly understood . . . those that the child is able to achieve and that the child might even enjoy working toward.

☆ There should be as few of them as possible.

Setting limits calls for experts. You are the experts.

Now, how do you carry these limits out?

8 / A Helping Hand

8/A Helping Hand

Your Job Description/

Taking care of your children *is* a long, hard, and demanding job. So is any rewarding job.

In our restaurant business, we trained our waitresses to be busy. When not waiting on customers, they were to complete other assignments: refilling supplies, dusting, straightening up.

Picture this situation. A waitress is dusting when a customer comes in. If she forgets her main reason for being there, she might consider the customer an interruption, instead of her primary responsibility.

A lifeguard may be sitting up in his lifeguard chair, comfortable and getting a nice tan. If a swimmer suddenly needs his help, the lifeguard shouldn't consider this some sort of interruption. These swimmers are his primary responsibility.

Parents need to consider children as their primary responsibility, not as interruptions.

Now . . . wait a minute. Parents have needs, too, don't they? They need time to fulfill their personal needs, don't they? Of course they do. So do waitresses, lifeguards, businessmen, coaches, athletes, secretaries, teachers, and everyone else.

Responsibility with appropriate authority *is* an important part of personal fulfillment. Creating the limits, revising them when necessary, expending the energy to work within the limits and interacting with one another *is* part of the joy of living.

Of course, there are coffee breaks, rest periods, substitutes, days off. Work takes energy. Interacting with people is tiring. There are good days and there are bad days. There are easy games and there are tough games. One day you have happy customers and another day it seems they are all grumpy.

Take the referee as an example. He keeps the game going smoothly. He is expected to call the plays according to the limits, to be impartial, consistent, and coolheaded. His job can be tough or easy on any given day. It depends on the mood of the players, their skill, the importance of the game, even the weather. Some days there are few close calls and few penalties. Other days, there can be some debatable, close calls and many penalties.

He rises to the demands of the game. He is in on every play. The game requires more or less of his effort, but the limits don't change. And refereeing doesn't interfere with his personal fulfillment. It's part of it. He doesn't bemoan the fact that he isn't a spectator. He relishes the job.

Like refereeing, guiding children can be a tough job or an easy job on any given day. It depends on the mood of the children, who they are with, the importance of the problems that come up, even the weather. Some days all goes smoothly. No one is stepping over the limits or challenging the calls. Other days you blow the whistle constantly and are called upon to make some debatable decisions.

But the limits don't change. You rise to the demands of the day. Guiding children isn't something that interferes with your personal life — it's part of it. The wholesome parent doesn't bemoan the job, but relishes it.

It goes back to a matter of the spirit. I am reminded of a pithy Bible passage:

> Whatever you do, work at it with all your heart, as working for the Lord, not for men, since you know that you will receive an inheritance from the Lord as a reward. It is the Lord Jesus Christ you are serving. Anyone who does wrong will be repaid for his wrong, and there is no favoritism (Col. 3:23-25).

How about a play on former President Kennedy's words: Ask not what the family can do for you; ask rather what you can do for the family.

If a businessman plays tennis, he must provide for the supervision of his business. If a parent plays tennis, he must provide for the supervision of his children. In either case, whether it be the businessman or the parent, the substitute supervisor is guided by the same limits you would use.

Let me return to my statement that parents have to consider children their primary responsibility, not interruptions. Gwen learned this:

"It hardly ever failed. All I had to do was to sit down for a TV show in the evening, and my five-year-old would come up asking me to read *The Lion, the Witch, and the Wardrobe*, or some other story book.

"I resented it — until I realized my TV watching was like the lifeguard getting a suntan. My primary responsibility was to the children.

"So I changed my viewpoint. If I sit down to watch a TV program with children around, I do so expecting to be interrupted. Sometimes I ask my child to wait, or offer some alternative activities until the program is over, or shift him over to dad. Most of the time, something works.

"Otherwise, I put off my TV watching until all the children are in bed — with one exception.

"Tuesday night at 8 o'clock. That is my favorite TV show. On that night my husband takes the major responsibilities of the evening so I can have that one pleasure . . . undisturbed and unbothered.

"Overall, my kids come first. I am their mother and want to be available."

Sam came to the same realization.

"The Saturday or Sunday football game would come on, and I'd sit down to watch it. Like clockwork, here would come my son Jeff, age five, with his football, wanting to play catch in the backyard.

"At first, it bugged me, and I tried to put him off. Then I realized *I had bought him* the football. Also, it was a chance to do some teaching.

"I'll play with you for fifteen minutes," I tell him now. That's about all his interest and energy span will allow for. It's time for fellowship and helping Jeff learn how to handle a football.

"So I start out my afternoons planning to play football in the backyard. After we're done and Jeff is tired or wants to go to another activity, I sit down and watch the rest of the game. Since the ball game lasts three hours, this doesn't always work out. Jeff may be back."

Let me toss in a serious question here. Am I asking parents to overindulge their children? Well, take a look at the last two examples. Both children involved are five-year-olds. You must do something with them, even if it interferes with your plans. They won't evaporate.

The presence or actions of a child demands a response whether you like it or not. I reported the choices Gwen and Sam made. Whatever you and your partner agree to do, well, do it with all your heart.

If you have any doubts about your choices, then consult with some parents whom you respect. The important point here is that your children are entitled to the best judgment available to you on their behalf and some serious, happy effort on your part in putting your judgment into action.

Enjoyable Parenthood

Isn't it strange that dedicated parents at times resist their job just as children resist limits? Half the battle in parenthood is accepting the task and the never-ending surprises and frustrations that children bring to the job.

To make parenthood easier and more enjoyable, here are five suggestions lumped together under a concept called help.

The Principle of Help

Help is assisting your child to get the best results from any effort put forth, and here are at least five ways of helping a child:

1. Redirecting unacceptable behavior.

2. Giving help as needed.
3. Giving more help than needed.
4. Preparing situations in advance.
5. Pressure.

Redirecting

I recall a scene in a friend's home.

There were four children in the television room, and the limit was . . . no horseplay. One of the smaller children was in an ugly mood that morning, and she was going around pestering the other children.

How should a mother handle that?

The little girl woke up in a bad mood and was making herself obnoxious. What was the simplest way to handle her?

She needed some help!

To swat her one would make a worse mess. So mother moved into the TV room and said: "Let's have some breakfast."

She bodily removed her daughter, plunked her in front of the table, and fed her something. All the girl needed was some help in behaving herself. Tomorrow she might be cooperative. Today she was a problem. Feeding her worked. If it hadn't, mother would have had to try something else.

Do you follow me? Parents have twenty years to raise children. You need not make a crisis on any one day.

This mother made her task as easy on herself as she could. She enforced the limit. The moody child was not allowed to bother the children in the television room. She simply was removed until she could get over her nasty mood: mother was redirecting unacceptable behavior.

Redirecting often is the answer to settling a dispute. If two children are fighting over a bicycle, the best solution might be redirecting their attention and energy somewhere else.

"Put the bike in the garage. Here's a football."

"Go and play ping pong."

If you are ready with a list of alternatives you make your job easier. This is redirecting.

Giving Help as Needed/

I was in a home one time . . . in the living room. A little boy was in the family room shouting: "I hate these filthy old things." We looked in to find a small child throwing blocks. He was frustrated because he couldn't stack them up.

His father moved in quickly and grabbed his hand, saying: "You can't throw blocks."

Then Dad quieted the boy down by just holding him. They sat on the floor together. Dad took two blocks and said: "Move the two closer together. Now you put one on top. Move it like this." He picked up four blocks for the child who then carried on himself, and we went back into the living room. No crisis.

Isn't that simple?

It's like the little girl pulling her wagon along the sidewalk, only to have it slip off and get stuck. The child begins to scream. Her mother comes on the scene, sees the problem and helps the child pull the wagon back up on the sidewalk, saying: "You got too close to the edge."

All the child needed was a little help, a single demonstration, some kind of explanation.

Erica is new in town, and it's hard to make friends. Her parents invited several families over for the evening and they played table games. It helped Erica get acquainted.

Help . . . giving help when needed.

Giving More Help Than Needed/

This type of assistance is given in spite of the fact the child can do the task. Just to make it more fun, the parent becomes a partner and pitches in with the child.

Loreen's family had a rule about the family room. She had to clean it up every night before she went to bed.

She could do the job by herself. She had the ability. Her father noted that the job was distasteful to Loreen, so he became her cleaning partner for a while. Together, they picked up the blocks, one holding the box, the other putting them in.

114

As a team, they stacked the books and put the toys in the toy box. They straightened up the rocking horse and put all the furniture in the proper position.

It was a fun time of the day — all because a father became a partner-parent. This help enabled a child to get personal pleasure as well as satisfaction from doing a job.

It is especially effective when a child faces jobs that are long and hard, or jobs that are scheduled at "tired" times of the day.

When Loreen's father first started helping her with the nightly pickup, he understandably picked up most of the debris. As the days went by, he picked up less and less.

Ultimately, all he needed to do every night was to remind her to pick up the family room. She breezed through the job by herself. Occasionally, he watched her or helped her.

Her father had helped Loreen keep the limits. Yet he avoided the rigidity of another father who had the same rule. Every night, he went flying through the house: "Where is that girl? She knows the limit is that she cleans up the family room every night. It's her responsibility. She's going to do it! Right now!"

This father wasn't being very creative. It is easy to see that this is not a helping atmosphere.

Preparing in Advance

This type of help is used by a parent who understands his child's abilities and limitations and anticipates when the child is ready for new experiences, even though the child isn't aware of them.

By making conditions favorable in advance, the parent helps the child discover new abilities. Such help may be unseen and even unknown by the child, but it often is most effective.

To prepare in advance, the parent must take his cues from his children. Watch your child for inclinations, interests, special abilities. From these, you decide how you are going to assist.

Through preparation in advance, you develop your child's abilities. You do this from day one. You can buy

115

crib toys and tie them to the crib so your baby can amuse himself.

Later on you decide your child may be interested in blocks. You buy some and put them out for him to play with. The same is done with crayons, push-pull toys, horses, other toys, and activities.

You watch for the developing interests of your child. You prepare the way for him.

Preparation in advance can guide a child's day. When a child wakes up, his blocks are set out for him. A book. A puzzle. You can guide your child's activity through this sort of help.

A Kind of Pressure/

Preparing conditions in advance can help in developing self-confidence in your child.

Purchasing a ball and bat and taking time to play with your child is an example. Providing a sewing machine and leaving easy projects around makes it easy for your daughter to get interested.

Leaving easy-to-read, interesting books around may stimulate reading. Leaving records of your choosing around may stimulate an interest in music.

Mr. Elgin noted his twelve-year-old boy was well-coordinated so he bought a ping-pong table and took time to teach his boy how to play.

Was he forcing something on his child? You might say so. He was teaching him a skill. When the social scene shifted to house parties, the boy would be ready on the basis of preference. He wouldn't have to worry about whether he would look silly in front of his friends.

"There's Nothing to Do!" /

Advance preparation helps the parent if he is ready with a list of suggestions. Sometime in your life you have heard these words (or will hear them): "Mom . . . I don't have anything to do?" A parent can be ready with several alternatives prepared and analyzed in advance.

"Why don't you go out and play on the swing?"
"I don't wanna."

"Why don't you go downstairs and play on the horse?"

"I don't wanna."

"Why don't you help me pick the colander clean?"

"I don't wanna."

"Why don't you go read one of your new *Little House* books?"

"Oh . . . O.K."

Advance preparation gives the child a choice. One father I talked to pointed out:

"I don't let my daughter go out with any non-Christians."

"Oh?"

"Right. And I don't let my daughter . . ."

On he continued until I got the impression — which turned out to be true — that he had given his daughter a list of activities she couldn't do. But he hadn't given her any suggestions on what she could do.

He hadn't done anything about providing her with some Christian boys to date.

The next time your teenager comes to you and grumbles: "Good grief! There's nothing to do around here. This place is dead!" What will be your reaction? Have a list of choices for him:

"Well, you can invite the youth group over
   Sunday."

"You can ride your bike."

"You can go to the YMCA."

"You can go to the gym."

"You can play ping-pong in the basement."

"You can play table games."

"You can invite your friends in."

"You can listen to records."

"You can put this kit together."

Pressure As Help /

At times, parents need to use pressure. It is time to go to church and your child doesn't want to go. It doesn't help much to say: "If you don't go, I'll whack you."

117

What kind of pressure gets him to church? You lock arms and march your child to the car. That's pressure.

"What do I do when my child sneaks out of church?" one parent asked. If they sneak out, then next time have them sit beside you. They'll probably say:

"What's the matter? Don't you trust me?"

The answer is: "No. I can't be sure what you will do when left out of my sight."

I was in a Sunday school department one day, where a little boy, ten or eleven years old, was throwing spit balls at some other children.

I heard the teacher say, "I wouldn't do that if I were you." The boy just ignored the teacher and kept up his activity.

Another adult, perhaps the superintendent, came in and observed what was going on. He moved in on the boy, sat him down in his chair and said:

"That's enough."

The boy looked up at the man and the man looked down at the boy. The little boy looked at his teacher, and his teacher looked at the man, who just shrugged his shoulders and walked away, but kept an eye on the boy.

The boy needed some pressure — some adult help. Even the child was smart enough to realize the man made a sensible decision.

The five techniques of help are valuable tools for you as you guide your children. An illustration of how these principles of help can be used over a period of years is Bill's use of the swimming pool as a tool in guiding his children as they grow up.

Bill had the pool built when his son was three years old. As soon as he could, he took his son to the pool and did everything he could to give him an understanding of the fun of swimming and water safety.

This is preparing in advance.

Over the years, Bill worked with the child, He taught his son how to float. How to swim. How to dive. He spent hours with him, showing him how, demonstrating, evaluating and correcting.

This is giving help when needed.

The best exercise from swimming comes to those who swim laps. Bill wanted his son to be a swimmer, not a soaker who just hangs around the side of the pool.

Good goal. Bill knew his son could swim laps. To encourage him, Bill joined his son in an effort to make the President's Fitness chart for fifty-mile swimmers. Together, they swam a half mile a day.

Next, they started compiling and comparing stopwatch times of their speed. All of this made the process more fun, and Bill's son became a very good lap swimmer.

This is giving more help than needed.

One day, Bill noticed that his son — now in junior high — was fooling around in the water much more than usual. There's nothing wrong with fooling around some of the time. But by watching, Bill noted that this fooling around was becoming a daily habit. The boy had obviously reached a plateau in his skills and interest in swimming.

So Bill came out to the pool a few days later with a mask, snorkel, and some fins. The boy was fascinated and so were his friends. Soon they were exploring all the aspects of skin diving, including underwater sea life. They were reading the encyclopedias about coral, sharks, and sting rays.

This was redirection as help.

Bill decided next that his son had ability to be a lifeguard. He had observed his son. He had spent enough time with him to know that he had the ability to become a lifeguard and that he would enjoy it. If his son took a lifesaving course, it would mature him, challenge him. Maybe he'd get a job and get some extra income for himself.

Bill suggested the boy take a course. He refused. Bill applied a little pressure.

"Son, I want you to take that course," he said, and took him to the YMCA and signed him up.

Bill's son took the course and passed.

This is pressure as help.

Bill had brought his son from an infant, helpless in the water, to a highly-trained aquatic expert. A complete educational process — all through the principles of help.

Redirecting often is the simplest way to handle unacceptable behavior and conflict between children.

Giving help as needed is the kind the child most frequently needs to accomplish a task.

Giving more help than needed probably is the most fun, where parent becomes partner. It insures personal pleasure and satisfaction while a child is doing a task.

Preparing in advance helps you keep a child busy or introduces him to new activities.

Pressure is the most dramatic and most often misunderstood. Yet it helps a child do what is expected of him, even if unpleasant, and ultimately encourages him in a path of independence. Use it carefully.

Loving guidance is rewarding both to the child and to the parent. Remember the promise:

> Train up a child in the way he should go and when he is old he will not depart from it (Prov. 22:6).

Help involves continuous daily effort. If you view each daily incident with your children as part of a twenty-year plan and not as a crisis of the moment, you have a good start on the proper use of help.

Lend your child a helping hand.

9 / Dealing With Resistance

9 / Dealing With Resistance

The Fact of Resistance

Question: How is it that our children resist some of our limits after we worked so hard to make them reasonable and reachable?

Why ask that question? Remember the essence of human nature:

All we like sheep have gone astray; we have turned every one to his own way (Isa. 53:6).

To elaborate a little on the characteristics of human nature, here is another biblical glimpse:

For rebellion is as the sin of divination, and stubbornness is as iniquity and idolatry (1 Sam. 15:23).

"I won't." Who hasn't responded this way? It's as though you were bewitched. In this mood, it's as though you idolized your own ideas and were ready to take on the whole establishment.

Limits reveal the spirit. They don't cause it.

It is normal and natural to want to do things the way you want to do them. A child is persistent in wanting to do what he wants to do.

Adults are the same way. How long must you supervise people in a business? As long as you have your business open. How long must you help people who have become resistant? As long as they are your responsibility. This is no problem to you if you accept the fact of resistance and accept the responsibility for dealing with it.

What limits do your children *want* to keep? This is not the question. The question is, What, in your considered judgment, is in the best interest of your children?

Today they will resist some limits and obey the rest. Tomorrow they may resist others and keep the ones they resisted yesterday.

Once a lady asked me:

"How do you get your children to do what you want them to do without getting angry at them?"

She had a ten-year-old daughter whose job was to carry out the milk bottles. Mother would wash the milk bottles and put them on the dish drainer. The little girl's job was to take the milk bottles out to the porch. Her mother would call out:

"The milk bottles are ready," in a nice voice. No child. She would call out again:

"The milk bottles are ready." (Nothing happened.) Then: "The milk bottles are READY!" Still no movement.

"DID you hear me? (Now at a shout.) The milk BOTTLES are READY!" (Still no child.)

By then, the mother told me, *I'm so mad I wipe my hands on my apron and go into the living room screaming:*

"YOU GET OUT THERE AND TAKE THOSE MILK BOTTLES OUT TO THE PORCH!!"

Then she does it. How do you get her to do it without getting so mad at her first?

I said: "Lady, do me a favor. Tomorrow night, when you wash the milk bottles, you call out just as nice as you know how: 'The milk bottles are ready' and then go after her." She did.

What a surprised child her daughter was. Imagine mother meaning what she says when she is in a good mood! What had happened here was that the little girl had discovered her mother wasn't serious until she was fighting mad. She didn't need to pay attention to her until then. This mother had a normal, natural problem — dealing with the resistance of her child to certain limits, and dealing with her own response to the child's resistance.

"Dad, You Should Take Better Care . . ."

Obviously, your children will not resist all limits. We had no problem with our son over his job of keeping the car clean. He wanted to keep the car clean. In fact, he was on my back:

"Dad, you should take better care of the car."

If we understand the nature of resistance, we will simply accept the responsibility for helping our children. One lady asked me:

"How do I get my daughter to stay home? I say to my daughter, 'I do not want you to go out tonight,' and she walks past me and out she goes. You just can't do anything with children these days. They won't listen to you. What do you do?"

The solution is simple. Get between her and the door. You need to help her stay home. You do not expect her to jump up and down with glee.

Your responsibility is to guide her in the way she should go. Your judgment will not necessarily be accepted by your child.

Reasons Don't Overcome Resistance

Your children will obey if you explain to them why you want them to do what you ask. Or at least that's what some people say.

Have you ever tried to explain to a child why it is in his best interests to stay home when he insists on going out?

Children could care less about your reasons when they want to get out. The smarter they are, the more ingenious they will be in trying to do what they want to do. At this point they don't want your attention. They want their own way and will do anything to get it.

What do they need?

They need a good-humored mother who appreciates the contest and enjoys it. They need a good-humored father who is backing her up and who steps in to help.

My Mom /

I can remember when I was a teenager attempting to talk my mother into letting me go out after she said I couldn't go.

I approached her something like this: "Aw, come on, Mom, won't you please let me go out? Please, Mom?"

I tried to make myself look and sound as pathetic as possible, appealing to her sympathy and her motherly instinct. Surely she would concede to someone as pleading as I was.

What do you do with a child who is playing the martyr? One who tries to put on a sincere act and tries to cajole something out of you that is against the limits?

She said: "No."

"Please, Mom, please let me go out!"

She said: "No." I decided there was no use being decent. It was necessary for me to try something else.

"So you say you love me, huh? How could any mother who loved her child treat me the way you are treating me? Can I go?"

She said: "No."

"But, Mom, everyone else but me is going. You wouldn't want to make a freak out of me, would you? Can I go?"

Once more . . .the same answer.

What else could I think of? You see, my objective was to get out of there. Anyway. Lie. Flatter. Whatever. But my best line was always the role of the victim. I figured my trump card was always:

"So you call yourself a Christian. How could any Christian mother treat me like this? Can I go?"

She didn't burst into self-defense. She had respect for my attempts to resist her plan. All she said was: "No."

That used to make me so angry! I used all the ingenuity and creativity I could come up with to make life miserable for my mother until I went to bed.

Sound familiar?

When I was defeated, I would go to bed, thinking:

How does a fellow get saddled with a parent like that? Boy, if only I would die, then she'd be sorry. ·

I pictured myself in a coffin . . . my mother looking down at my dead body. In my imagination, I fired this thought off toward my grieving mother:

Serves you right!

There was no point in appealing to Dad. He would just back Mom up.

But in my better moments I was aware that they loved me. I sensed an attitude of approval and a real affection for me.

I grew up, was married, and had some children.

Guess what? Right. To my amazement, I heard some of the same reasoning come out of the mouths of my own children. I found myself interfering with the wishes of my children. And they were saying the same things I said to my mother. The same things your children are saying . . .

"Look what you are doing to me! A nice lady like you. You want to ruin my life?"

What your children want so fervently isn't always what they need. You need to respect their wants. But their wants, according to your judgment, may not be in their best interests.

It's up to you.

Affection

The Bible says it so simply:

> Be devoted to one another in brotherly love. Honor one another above yourselves (Rom. 12:10).

Dealing with resistance will reveal your spirit. It is better to back away from a rebellious child if you cannot deal with him affectionately. Take care of your own spirit first. Then come back at resistance.

A child's behavior doesn't determine your sense of success; affectionate firmness backed by carefully thought-through conviction and the backing of your partner does. To illustrate:

A Fighting Lightweight

I once observed raw human nature in the living

room of a lovely home. A four-year-old was pounding a three-year-old over the head. No adult had heard what went on before the beating started, so no one knew what led up to the fight. At a time like this, you never find out who started the fight. It is almost impossible. So this is no time for a lecture or questioning. A swift rescue operation is called for. The mother did just that. She moved in without a word and hauled the four-year-old off his victim and took him into the kitchen.

"I hate you," he screamed at his mother. "Leave me alone."

Mother coolly replied: "I know you feel that way, but until you cool off you cannot play with your sister, and I'll just wait here until you do."

This is where it all starts . . . affection . . . affection that portrays a tenderness, kindness, gentleness *no matter what the behavior.*

By affection, I do not mean indulgence, letting children run wild, ruining things, or hitting each other. It is just that when you deal with children it must be done with a basic gentleness and firmness.

Sometimes neighbors must work together. In this case, one little neighbor girl was a biter. You can't order a small child to stop biting. She was playing in the backyard with the child next door. There was a blood-curdling scream and both mothers came running out of their houses. Sure enough. The neighbor girl had been bitten. The children were fighting over the swing.

The neighbor girl had tried to take over, and the child next door resisted. Biting is a powerful weapon and she used it. She knew she had done wrong.

One mother hurried to the bitten child to comfort her. The other mother hurried to the one who had done the biting and took her into the house. She said:

"You forgot, didn't you?"

"Yeah, I did," the girl replied.

In this case, the little girl was already sorry, and the mother's approach was much more effective than if she had glared at the child and said:

"You little brat. I'll pound you for doing that."

Her mother went on to remind her child that mothers are there to help.

The storm was over. There is no simple solution to such a problem. It takes patience and closer watching by both mothers. In an hour, the children were playing in the sandbox with one of the mothers watching.

In a year the problem had disappeared.

See what I mean? I am not suggesting that you let your children run wild. You can deal with your child's most obnoxious behavior in a gentle but firm way.

There is a difference between gentle firmness and hostile firmness. A basic affection for the child, no matter what the behavior, is an important building block to parental success.

The Proper View of Resistance

Resistance will take a number of directions. A child is purposeful about carrying out his own plans. Resistance might take the form of crying, temper tantrums, sloppiness, pitting parents against each other.

This interplay between the ingenuity and intelligence of a child as it attempts to deal with parents is what makes parenthood interesting.

It is a lifelong challenge and should be viewed as an exciting day-by-day way of life. A sort of *very* positive us-looking-after-their-best-interests type of thing.

Resistance should be viewed as normal. Parents need to respect the determination of their children. Children have their own plans . . . their own ideas. We appreciate their ingenuity and intelligence — and their need for the Spirit of God.

The Neighbor Girl

It was a typical day when I pulled my car into our driveway and walked into the living room — only to find a neighbor girl playing in our house. She had blocks all over the living room.

Which was fine.

We enjoyed having the neighborhood children

over, and they were welcome to play with the blocks. After a while, our little guest announced:

"I'm going home."

The blocks hadn't been picked up. And one of the rules at our house was that when the children finished playing with toys, they picked them up and put them away. So I said:

"Pick up the blocks first."

The limits at our house applied to everyone. Children. Parents. Even guests. But this child didn't see it that way.

"I won't pick up the blocks," she announced, and headed for the closet to get her coat. This was resistance to our limits — limits that my wife and I had agreed on. Yet it was resistance that can be expected. What do you do when a child won't go along with the limits? You help her.

To give her some help, I had to catch her on her way to the closet and then drag her, kicking and screaming, back to the living room.

"Leave me alone," she screamed, still fighting.

This girl really needed help. What she did not need at this time was a lecture on respect for adults. All I needed to do was quietly help her. With my hand over hers, we started picking up the blocks. I wasn't doing it *for* her. I was helping her live within the limits. She tried a new approach.

"Leave me alone. I'll do it myself."

That's O.K. So I left her alone. As soon as I did, she took off for the closet.

Now . . . that's resistance.

So I caught her again and dragged her back into the living room. That's what's known as helping her.

She tried another tactic. She just stood there, waiting for me to pick up the blocks. But I wasn't about to do her job for her. I respected her ability to do this too much to take the job on myself.

What I *was willing to do* was to help her. So with my hand over hers, we resumed picking up the blocks.

Finally, we were finished. She looked up at me and said:

"I'm going home and tell my mother on you, and I

130

am never coming back." And she gave me a final, dirty look as she went her way.

From her parting remarks, you would have thought I'd made a mortal enemy. But no. She came back to our house again and again.

The reason was simple. At her house, there were no boundaries. If she yelled loud enough or cried long enough, or made herself obnoxious enough, she could always end up getting her way.

As a result, the poor child was lost. She liked our house because there were boundaries there.

The Boy Who Hid

This incident was shared with me by a friend of mine. It occurred at a national children's conference where around 300 children between the age of two and twelve attended. The first day about forty of the younger children expressed themselves as only children can that *they didn't want to be separated from their bigger sisters and brothers.*

With a little bit of discussion, all of them were convinced to go with their age groups. All of them, that is, except for one rather large seven-year-old who survived "the cut" and hid out with his nine-year-old sister until the fourth day of the conference when she finally tired of his dogging her every step and blew the whistle on him.

The leader of the six and seven-year-olds was alerted, but when she came to pick him up, the truant boy hung on to a handy post and began screaming.

"Oh, never mind," the teacher said. Then turning to the boy she added: "But tomorrow you report to your group." The next day he did so. And the crisis seemed to have been averted. That is, until midway through the final day, when the first and second graders on a picnic suddenly crossed paths with the third and fourth graders who were preparing for a greased pig chase.

Before the teacher could say "porky," the boy infiltrated the older group and disappeared as slickly as the slippery sow.

The teacher spotted the boy running — right behind his sister — and she called for me to help.

131

I hoped there would be no resistance this time, for parents of most of the children were lining up at a nearby building for a meeting. Fortunately, I caught up with the group before the boy saw me coming. I put my arm around the boy and started leading him back toward his proper group.

He was all cooperation until he suddenly lunged toward a nearby swing set and entwined himself around a post. As I approached him, he started screaming at the top of his voice:

"I don't want to go! I don't want to go!"

Everyone turned to watch — the children chasing the pig — the parents lining up for the meeting — the other children about 100 yards away at their picnic.

What do you do with a child who is putting on a scene?

He hung on to that swing post as if his body had sprouted fifty suction cups. Finally, I was able to pry loose one arm.

Then the other arm. The legs were the most difficult, but finally, the screaming, kicking mass of boy was all mine.

Even though I had to really bear down with all I had to hold him, I smiled at him and said:

"You'll really enjoy what we have planned for you today." He began calming down, and 100 yards later he was a different boy. No more screaming. No more kicking. He gladly took his Kool-Aid and cookies. Then he asked:

"Do you know what my name is?"
"No, but I would like to."
"It's Bryan."
"I'm glad you told me that."
"Do you know where I live?"
"I'd like to."

"I live in Ohio. Look here at this ring I've got . . ."
Again, approval . . . affection . . . respect. Help is not enough. Help is effective only if the other three are present.

We were great friends the rest of that fifth and final day. I had only one regret. I wish Bryan had been found out the first day instead of the next to last. I think we would have had a great time together that week.

Summing Up

Setting limits brings out human nature — which is to resist some limits. This is normal and to be expected. It's normal, but not spiritual.

Accordingly, parents have two jobs to do:

1. To see to it that children stay within reasonable limits in spite of their resistance.

2. To point our children Godward — He alone can help them with self-centeredness, rebellion, and stubbornness.

10 / Supervision

10 / Supervision

Put 'Em All Together

Setting limits . . . dealing with resistance . . . giving help. Put them together and give them one name.
That name would be supervision.

A Championship Coach

Supervision should be considered a positive activity. Let me tell you about my basketball coach.

We had a championship team one year because we had a championship coach. All of us on the team regarded him with admiration, affection, and good will. Occasionally, we dreaded him.

For me, it was when he watched me practice.

A player wants to look good when the coach is watching. My thought whenever he was looking at me in practice was to get the ball and take a hook shot. This was the best part of my game.

Did that satisfy him? No. He always came up with the same dreaded sentence:

"Good shot. Now let me watch you dribble."

Dribbling was the worst part of my game. If you were to describe me as a basketball player, you would say my footwork was good, my teamwork was good, my passing

137

was good, and my shooting was good. But what did the coach concentrate on?

My dribbling!

It wasn't as though he didn't know about my abilities. We agreed I was a good basketball player. One must be to play on a championship team.

He was a wise coach, quietly watching and firmly insisting on correcting the weak side of my game and developing the strong side. Before the year was up, I became a good dribbler.

To deal with the negative is positive.

What the Boss Inspects

There is a saying in the business world: "The employee will do what the boss *inspects*, not what he expects."

In the restaurant business, the job of the supervisor requires him to meet prearranged labor costs, food costs, standards of cleanliness, and more. This is not optional. This is his work — full-time.

My coach had learned that a basketball player will do what the coach *inspects*, not what he expects.

Parents, too, quickly learn that a child will do what a parent *inspects*, not what he or she expects. Like the supervisor of a business, or the coach, a parent must be continuously and directly involved in *making* things happen. Some limits are easily achieved and require little attention. Others demand constant attention and effort.

You Gotta Believe!

There was a phrase that we introduced back in the first part of the book. It is "confident expectation." *Supervision involves confident expectation.*

It is assumed that you are doing something or requiring something you believe is worthwhile and in the best interest of your child. If so, you will have enough conviction to see it through, confidently expecting the child to appreciate your efforts in the long run.

In other words, you gotta believe! In your plan!

Weekend at the Lake/

Supervision begins with an adult decision. Recently, we met a family at a conference in Wisconsin. Since they were returning from the conference to Toronto and would travel near our summer cabin on Lake Michigan, we invited them to spend a few days with us.

We extended the invitation without realizing what turmoil it would cause the family. The problem was this: the family was traveling to Toronto, where the grandparents of the two children lived. And who doesn't look forward to getting back with grandpa and grandma?

Then along we came with our invitation. So the dad announced: "We're going to stop at the Brandts on the way."

It's a very scenic spot. It has all kinds of facilities. Good food. Great view of a big lake. Sunshine. Games. Happy combination between camping out and comfort.

You'd expect cheers, right? Well, that's not what echoed through the car when the announcement was made.

"You never heard such a hue and cry," the dad recounted to me. "They wanted to go to grandpa's and grandma's right now. And that was that."

Wisely, the mom and dad didn't make a big issue out of it. There were no big arguments, no yelling to the kids to stop their protesting. No big confrontation. Just:

"Well, we're going to do it. And I think you'll really enjoy it."

When the family pulled up to the beautiful lakeshore cabin, the children were resentful and skeptical about the events of the next two days.

However, the following Monday you could hardly drag the kids away — even though it was time to leave for their grandparents' house.

The parents' plan formed a foundation for supervision. They stuck to the plan with the confident expectation that the children would benefit, knowing the children and the fun awaiting them.

From Sandbox to Curfew/

Supervision assures staying within boundaries. A

lady put her toddler in a sandbox with a little shovel and went into the house.

"Now, you stay there till I come back."

A while later, she came back out, only to find the child digging in her flower bed. She discovered that she must either watch to make sure the child stayed in the sandbox or find a way to protect her flowers. Respect for flowers is too much to ask of a toddler.

One of the most important helps I believe we gave our teenagers was to see that one of us was there when our children came home after being out at night.

They didn't like it. But when your children realize you will be there when they come home, it is quite an encouragement to observe limits. They would often say:

"Why are you always waiting for me?" The answer was simple:

"We love you. We are interested in you. We want to know what you have been doing, that's all. We want to make sure you got home when you said you would."

The older your children become, the more they need your personal supervision and the more they will resist it. I have seen teenagers get into trouble because their parents allowed them to have a party at their house and the parents took off, leaving them unsupervised. Your personal supervision removes temptations.

Reducing the Odds

In supervising, a parent follows up on limits. For example, a child asks her mother for permission to go out.

"Sure," Mom replies, "if you promise to be home at 10:00." The daughter agrees but does not show up on time.

"I wish you would listen to me," says the mother. "It's in your best interest to come home at 10:00."

"Yes, Mom. I just forgot."

"OK. Now, next time come in at 10:00."

The child decides she has a 50-50 chance of getting away with it the next time. A 50-50 chance is worth gambling on. So the child tries it again and comes home a little later the next time.

140

This time, the parents aren't even there. The child slips into the house and says:

"Whew, I got away with that one."

The next time she goes out, she figures she has a 60-40 chance of getting away with staying out late. She comes in at 10:45. Mother gives her another lecture about coming home on time. Ultimately, the girl realizes that if she can just put up with the lecture every time, she can set her own time for coming in.

Better not to set a limit if you don't intend to enforce it.

The Girl and Her Snowsuit

I once was supervisor of some cooperative nursery schools where parents could learn about preschool children by assisting a professional staff. One day I visited the nursery school. It was winter time. When children went outside to play, they were required to wear their snowsuits.

I came into the yard, and all the children but one were in the snowsuits. Where was her snowsuit? It was draped over the arm of the lady who was watching her.

"Why doesn't that child have her snowsuit on?" I asked the lady.

"She won't let me put it on her," the lady said. Now, think about that. Here is this grown lady buffaloed by a little child.

"Let me watch you try it," I suggested. The lady approached the girl in a frightened, gingerly manner and said: "Would you like to put your snowsuit on?"

"No," answered the little girl quickly.

"See?" said the lady as she turned to me. I asked for the snowsuit.

"Let me show you how to put it on." I took the snowsuit, caught the child, and as she was pulling away from me and resisting violently, I got one arm into a sleeve and the other arm into the other sleeve.

To my embarrassment I realized that is not how you put on snowsuits — but at least I was doing something. I was trying. I started over again and got one leg in and the other leg in, and finally — gasp — both arms. The child was tugging and fighting me every inch of the way. I zipped her up.

The girl gave me one final dirty look and then suddenly ran off to play.

The teacher's aide looked at me as though I were a miracle man. What did I do? I did what I needed to do to help that child into her snowsuit. Did that child need a snowsuit? Yes. Did I do a bad thing? No. I did the child a favor.

I was just following up on a good limit — with the use of a little pressure.

Sometimes . . . Pressure

Sometimes, you must use pressure in your supervision. Children resist in all kinds of ways. For example, there is the question of church. What do we do about our children going to church?

My wife and I decided it was in the best interest of our children to go to church twice every Sunday and once every Wednesday. They had contrary opinions at times, but this was the considered judgment of my wife, the world's greatest expert on the subject of our children. It was also my opinion. The only question we had was how do we get them there?

Children have comments about church, such as "wait until I turn eighteen and I will never darken a church door again." "You make me go to church, and you will regret it." We heard all the standard threats that you have heard or will hear. In our judgment (yes — in our plan), church is good for one, and the question of whether to go was debatable, but not negotiable. They could say anything they wanted.

One day, one of our children announced just before the midweek service:

"I am not going."

So we had to help her get there. How do you do that? First, we helped her with her shoes. When a teenager doesn't want shoes on, it takes two of you to put them on. But between my wife and myself — and we worked hard at it — we put her shoes on.

142

The next step was to get her moving. We had to get her up but discovered her knees wouldn't work. We worked at that problem for a while, solved it, only to find out she had a broom up her back.

Next, with my arm locked in hers she was walking stiff-legged, shouting:

"I won't . . . I won't . . . I won't . . . I won't!"

It is difficult to get a person outside when her knees won't work and her back won't bend. It is especially difficult to get her into the car. But we got her in. We drove to the church and one of her girl friends was standing there on the curb. That girl friend had no idea how we got our daughter there. They immediately walked off, chatting happily together.

All our daughter had needed was a little help . . .

You say, what did you do about it after that? We didn't do anything about it. She needed some help, and we gave it to her. That was the end of it.

After church, she came up and said:

"What do you say we stop and get an ice cream sundae on the way home?"

Well, why not? If I were to deprive her of one, I would deprive myself of one. I didn't do anything wrong. Neither did she, really. She needed some persistent supervision with the confident expectation on our part that we were doing our daughter a favor.

"But won't you turn your children against church?" you ask.

Isn't it strange. People will ask that question but they don't have the same sort of concern about school.

Do you have any doubts about whether your children will reject school? When our children resist school, the only question is how to get them there. Do you have any doubt about whether or not your children should visit a doctor?

One of our children didn't like doctors. When she needed medical attention I had to scoop her up, kicking and screaming, plunk her in the car and drag her into the doctor's office and hold her down.

There were occasions when the nurse sat on one end of that child, and I sat on the other, while the doctor let her have it with a needle. She was screaming.

Is that any way to treat a child? It certainly is. If I love my child, and that child needs medical attention, the only question in my mind is *how* to get her there — not *should* I!

None of our children has rejected doctors. None of our children has rejected education. They all went through college. None of them has rejected the church.

What Do You Do With a Charging Teenager?

We had this experience one time. Our son decided he was going out. We had told him he wasn't going out. He said he was and headed for the door.

So what do you do in such a situation?

I took the advice I had given other parents and got between him and the door.

He decided to remove me from the door. As he approached, I looked him over. He was almost as tall as I was and in better shape. He needed a lot of help that night. A lot of supervision.

We were both pretty tired before the evening was over.

Now you say, won't that shape his destiny forever after? I think it helped. What did it do? It proved we would do everything we could to make happen what we thought was the best for him.

This is the same son who is now a Ph.D. . . . a college professor.

If doing your best to guide your children is the worst criticism a child has of his parents, that's not too bad. Your judgment might be a little faulty along the way, but there is no question about your intent or your effort. There is no question about your attitude or your dedication to your children's best interests.

You must be convinced that what you are doing is in the best interest of your child. Confident expectation. Of course, you need to be kind . . . respectful . . . affectionate . . . evidencing an attitude of approval. . . and be decent about it.

144

Pressure. Occasionally, it's necessary in supervision. Pressure is a force. The stronger the pressure, the greater the danger of misuse — and the need for mixing pressure with affection and patience.

The Slide

Supervision involves demonstration. You are observing your children and some of their friends on the playground. One says:

"Hey, I'm going to try out the slide."

Another: "Hey, me too!"

Just like that everyone discovers the slide and converges on it at once. They knock each other down and push some children to the back of the crowd.

So you go over and pick out two or three of the children.

"Now, Wanda is going to go first. Then Mike will go next. After Mike is Joe." You line them up. You show them how to take turns.

So what happens the next time this phenomenon occurs? You guessed it. Everyone converges on the slide again — at once. Kids tumble everywhere. They trample on each other.

You have to demonstrate again. And maybe again and again. But children will learn as you demonstrate. You must work at it. Cooperation doesn't come naturally.

Too Much Time?

I can almost hear you saying:

"You've got to be kidding! Do all that? Spend that much time?"

Well . . . yes. That is, if you want to put together that perfect play.

Look at the area of eating. When you first begin your child on the process of eating, she can't even find her own mouth. She can't even get her index finger and her thumb to coordinate.

So you stick a bottle in her mouth. Or a spoonful of baby food. Next, you get her in a highchair and put a little food on her tray. You show the child how to eat the food and then watch what she does.

If she throws the food all over the kitchen, you guide her hand to the food and back into her mouth. After doing that, you again let her experiment.

Little by little, you progress. Finally, she's interested in a spoon. So you help her spoon the food into her mouth. Then, you allow her to experiment with the spoon for a while.

Even after she masters a spoon, it will be a while before she can handle a fork and a knife.

Keep the drama in perspective. It is an educational process. Each spill, each messed tablecloth, each soiled outfit is a part of that process. It takes a few years.

Alfred and Jerry

Supervision involves a lot of time. It involves staying with the job.

Roxanne was trying to teach her two sons to share. She started the process with a truck.

"Alfred has been playing with the truck. Now, it's your turn, Jerry."

Jerry started playing with the truck, and Roxanne left, feeling the sharing pattern was complete. She had hardly left the room when a cry broke out. Alfred had crowned Jerry and snatched back the truck.

Roxanne started the process all over again. She realized she had to stay closer and supervise the process longer this time.

It took a lot of effort and constant watching to keep her two boys out of each other's hair. There was no such thing as a short cut. Sharing doesn't come naturally.

Why? Because of human nature.

> All we like sheep have gone astray; we have turned every one to his own way (Isa. 53:6).

This tendency is seen most clearly in small children. They don't hesitate to attack each other to get what is wanted. To expect them to share eagerly is too much to ask of small children.

Larrrr – e-e-e-e-e!

When our children were small we had to make a choice. Would we raise grass or children in our backyard? We decided we would raise children instead of grass. We discovered that if you want children in your backyard, you won't have much competition from the neighbors. So the neighborhood children played in our backyard. We liked that, because we knew where our children were and we could keep an eye on them.

One day I was watching some children play in the backyard. Across the ether waves came this voice. There is one of these, I suppose, in every neighborhood. It sounded something like this:

"Laaaarrrrrr-e-e-e-e-e-e!"

Larry kept right on playing. The call came a second time. Then a third time. Everyone in the block could hear it. One of the children near him said:

"Hey, Larry, don't you know your mother's calling you?"

"I don't need to go yet," Larry said. Then we heard a short, crisp voice:

"Larry!"

Away he went. You see, his mother had two voices. He knew perfectly well that when his mother used that first voice she wasn't about to do anything about it, except make a lot of noise. She should have used her second voice the first time.

Children learn to adjust to mother's screaming. Be consistent. It even helps save energy.

The Supervisors

There are two supervisors in a family — Mom and Dad. Supervision involves commitment of both parents to the same limits. Setting limits is not an arena for unresolved arguments between parents. Your style of leadership may be different, but the limits must be the same.

Who is the final, ultimate authority when it comes to supervision? The wife may well have the most knowledge and experience, so the husband should consider carefully before he overrules his wife. He, however, is the final authority.

This all changes if the wife works or has many outside activities. Careful planning over the division of responsibilities is obvious. A strategy for the various trouble spots — bedtime, meals, getting to school, going to church, activities, TV rules (all potential brushfires) — saves many debates between parents and gives the children a sense of stability and family cooperation.

Supervision in the family involves your personal presence just as surely as the supervision of a business or the coaching of a team.

IV / Building Your Child's Life

11 / The Truth About Consequences

11 / The Truth About Consequences

We Sow What We Reap/

We do our children a great favor if we help them understand there are consequences for their actions . . . good and bad.

> Do not be deceived: God cannot be mocked. A man reaps what he sows. The one who sows to please his sinful nature, from that nature will reap destruction; the one who sows to please the Spirit, from the Spirit will reap eternal life. Let us not become weary in doing good, for at the proper time we will reap a harvest if we do not give up (Gal. 6:7-9).

A boy was spending the summer on his uncle's farm and found those verses to be literally true. It was a picturesque place, complete with sparkling river rolling through the farm and a friendly country store just down the road.

Among the chores the boy was assigned during the summer was the planting of a bean patch. The farmer took the boy out to the patch, where he had carefully spaded up rows and rows of nicely spaced holes in which to plant the beans.

"Now, remember, you are to put only four or five seeds in every one of the hills," the uncle told the boy when he left.

The boy started on the job. He carefully put four or

153

five beans in each one of the holes. He finished the first row . . . the second row . . . a third row.

But his dedication began to wither in the heat of the sun. And there was that inviting river just fifteen or twenty yards away.

Finally, the boy made a decision no experienced farm boy would have made. He decided that if he would put more beans in each hill he would get done sooner.

So he upped the number from five to ten. The job started going faster — but not fast enough. He started dumping entire handfuls of beans into each hill. Finally he couldn't stand it any more.

He dumped all of the remaining beans in the last two hills, covered all those empty hills and left.

He headed for the house, jumped into his bathing suit, and started for the river, when he met his uncle.

"Finished already?" the uncle asked.

"Yeah, it was easy."

"I've never known anyone to plant a bean patch so fast," said the uncle. But he let the matter drop.

A few weeks later the boy reaped what he had planted. He was in the house, when his uncle rousted him out.

"Hey, your beans are starting to come up. Let's go out and take a look at them."

Together the boy and his uncle went out to inspect the job. There they were — an incredible looking bunch of beans.

A few rows were just fine . . . four or five sprouts coming from every hill. Suddenly, the hills were sprouting ten plants. And the final row had so many bean sprouts fighting with each other from each hill you could hardly count them.

The boy, in the fourth grade then, has never forgotten his experience. He didn't realize what he had done because he hadn't grown up on a farm. No knowledgeable farm boy would have been so stupid. He would have known the consequences of such planting.

You reap what you sow.

Girls in Trouble

I have had distraught parents come to me and plead: "Please, Dr. Brandt, could you help us break up this romance between our daughter and her boyfriend? They have very little in common and are both immature. They insist on getting married."

Then comes the same dreary answers to my questions:

"How long have they been dating?"

"About ten months."

"If this match has been acceptable for ten months, what's wrong with it now?" I ask.

"It hasn't been acceptable, but we didn't want to upset our daughter or appear narrow-minded. We had hoped something would happen to break it up."

These parents are reaping consequences. They made a decision the opposite of their best judgment. Obviously, your children will marry someone they know. So you need to be careful who they know.

Another set of parents came in with their pregnant daughter.

"I told her she was seeing too much of that boy," wails the mother, "but she wouldn't listen.

"She would say: 'Mother, don't you trust me?' I wanted my daughter to know I trusted her, and look what happened."

What happened? The normal consequences of allowing a young couple too much unsupervised freedom. They had no more conception of the consequences of their behavior than the fourth-grade boy had when he was planting beans.

"What can I do?" pleaded another mother. "My daughter parks in front of the house in a car with her boyfriend for an hour or two night after night. She refuses to come in."

" 'Why are you so suspicious, Mother?' she says. 'You don't need to worry about us.' "

If you ask me, the parents should do something. There *is* a basis for concern. Her daughter surely isn't re-

155

viewing Bible verses night after night for an hour or two out there. We all know what goes on in a parked car in the dark. But how do you get the daughter out of the car?

There is only one way that I know of. Help her out. How do you do that? You go outside, open the car door, reach in, and drag her out.

But won't that embarrass her?

Yes, it will. This is the consequence of defying you. Won't she be angry? She will be furious. This is her problem.

What if she doesn't come home and parks somewhere else? Then don't allow her to go out. You may also need to deal with the boy and/or his parents.

Remember, this is your beloved daughter. But the ecstasy of physical closeness at her age is too tempting for her to handle. She needs your help. The boy needs his parents' help. The consequences of ignoring your parental responsibility at this time can be a poorly matched marriage, or, to say the least, allowing behavior that your child knows to be risky and degrading. The parents of teenage boys should know where their boys are and cooperate with the girls' parents.

At this stage, your children need your guidance and help the most. They will appreciate it five years later. Don't expect anything but resistance now.

Remember the story of the fourth-grade boy on the farm? The farmer left the boy unsupervised and so did the parents of these girls and boys. So the children were allowed to make foolish choices.

Limits Never Cease

Life has its consequences. Harsh and cruel though they may be, we must prepare our children for them.

This is what one dad was trying to prepare his boy for when he wrote him the following letter at his college graduation:

Dear Son:

I'm sure you are thrilled by the idea of taking your place at last in adult affairs – a station of life you probably look upon as a time when "big people" will stop telling you to do things . . . or not to do things. Your dad has found out that the

156

chains of adult life are wrought of stiffer stuff than the feeble fetters of childhood.

Believe me, no one ever suffered a furrowed brow from such simple commands as "Eat your cereal" . . . "Do your homework" . . . "Report for band practice." What once may have seemed a terribly harsh order, "Put away your comic book," will pale into insignificance when compared with an order from the doctor: "Cut out all pastries and sweets." The bigger you get the bigger other people seem to get – if not bigger in stature, then bigger in authority. For example, did you see the look on Dad's face when the Internal Revenue man ordered him to report to the collector's office with last year's tax receipts? When a traffic officer says, "Pull over to the curb," Dad pulls. When grandmother says, "Roll up the window," Dad rolls up. I just want to prepare you for a lifetime of saying, "Yes, sir," to master sergeants, shop foremen, loan company executives, bank tellers, tradesmen, public officials, car dealers, game wardens, and a host of other people you never dreamed were your superiors. Even the most politely phrased commands like "Please remit," or "Kindly step back in the bus," are still commands.

Ushers will order you down an aisle; headwaiters will tell you where to sit; courts will summon you for jury duty; the city hall will notify you to shovel the snow off your sidewalk.

You will be dragged off to parties at other people's houses and dragged out of bed by people who come to your house. You will be kept off the grass by policemen and kept up by weekend guests. You will be put on committees and put off buses. This is the true life beyond commencement. Congratulations and good luck.

Dad

P.S. Get a haircut.

A Bad Break . . . Or?/

In life you get some tough breaks and some good breaks. Either way, you take the consequences.

A young athlete grabbed all the football headlines in high school and went off on a scholarship to a university. There he did very well his first year.

The consequences of that were praise, newspaper headlines, girls wanting to date him, parties.

How did he react to his consequences? He reacted by not doing his schoolwork. The result: he became ineligible to play football.

He enjoyed the acclaim all right, but he didn't like the consequences of his choice of not studying. He blamed other people for his choice. He tried to make his teachers out as being down on him, but he really didn't do any studying. So the consequences of that choice were that he disappeared from sight and dropped out of school, griping all the way about what a tough break he got. He became a bitter kid running away from reality. He wasn't ready to take the consequences of life . . . the good with the bad.

Another athlete had the same choices. He went to college to get an education *and* play baseball. He made good grades *and* starred on the diamond with his outstanding ability.

He concentrated on his studies first and was so good that he was encouraged to enroll in a dental school, which he did.

He was such a good player, however, that he was signed by a championship major league ball team. He became a star with the team, and he still kept at his dental school studies, attending in the off-season.

After he retires from professional baseball, he will have a career ahead of him in dentistry.

Two athletes. Both had the same choices. Both received the consequences of their choices. Both were rewarded.

Different Ways . . ./

Our job as parents is to head our children in the

right direction. To do that, we need to give some thought to the kind of consequences that will help them along the way.

Some people call them rewards . . . or punishment. I like to think of them all as consequences — good and bad. We make the choices and suffer or enjoy the consequences.

Adults know that the consequences of getting good grades are a better chance to get a job or into college, and good grades usually result in more knowledge about life.

The consequences of learning to be cooperative are leadership positions, promotions, raises.

The consequences of poor grades and poor cooperation are trouble and missed chances, difficulty in getting a job, difficulty in getting into school.

Such remote objectives as college, jobs, promotions, and raises are hardly of interest to children. But as adults, we know these are real. We know that our choices and experiences have their consequences. Even someone else's choices can affect us. For example, we all know of people who suffered terrible bodily injury and financial reverses because a drunk driver ran into their car.

I have a friend who lost his business because he guaranteed someone else's notes. The notes were defaulted, so the bank came after my friend.

There is not much point in lecturing our children about consequences they can't understand, but we can teach them on their own level.

If you don't study, you can't go out to play.

If you don't practice, you don't make the team.

Announcing consequences and making them stick is one form of help.

You force your child to study, and the reward is he gets to play outside.

You make your boy practice, and the reward is he makes the team.

You make your child come to the table, and the reward is he gets to eat.

It's a twenty-year process.

If you allow your boy to use the car, and he brings it back in good shape, you can be lavish with your praise. If he doesn't — using too much gas or driving too far — he should suffer the consequences. He pays for the gas or maybe gives up his next turn to use the car.

Actually, you as a parent aren't as concerned with the single issue. You're teaching him that his choices have consequences.

If your child goes out and goes where she said she would go and with whom, then you are lavish with your praise. If she doesn't go where she promised or come back when she said she would, there should be some consequence to face. You make her pass up the next event at school. Again, it's the learning experience, not the incident, that you capitalize on.

If a child takes good care of his bike, he is entitled to your praise. If he doesn't, he must do so or he gets grounded for a day.

If a child eats her food and has good table manners, she enjoys the family fellowship and food. If not, she leaves the table or goes without dessert.

Say a child refuses to eat. Well, one way to handle him is through some judicious starvation. In other words, don't let him eat between meals. He'll find that if he doesn't eat and isn't allowed to eat between meals, the consequence is hunger.

Suffering consequences helps a child get a proper picture of reality.

Teach Consequences by Observing Others

There are other ways of teaching consequences. You will not let your child ruin his bike to learn a lesson. But you can point out to your child how the neighbor boy ruined his bike because he didn't take care of it.

"You know Sam always wants to borrow your bike. It's because he ruined his. You haven't."

Nor do you let a little toddler wander out into the street and get hit to learn the consequences. You just don't allow him. But you can point out a dead animal beside the road and tell the child why it was killed.

A teenager can't understand why you don't let him run around with undesirable friends. There are reasons. No sense letting a child learn the hard way on something like that which could lead to a pregnancy, trouble with the law, arrests, etc.

But you can point out what happened in other children's lives.

One night there was a terrible crash down the street from our house. So we ran down to the corner, and saw two cars completely mangled and four young people equally broken up.

They had been playing chicken with the cars, seeing who would veer away first. They came to the corner and neither driver would give in.

We used that as a teaching situation. Here were young people who had access to a car and all the freedom they wanted. A half year later, one of them was still in the hospital.

There was a boy who could get his way by being cantankerous, uncooperative, and obnoxious. He applied his usual sullen techniques to his father when he became a teenager and got a fast car, because his father was trying to make him cooperative and unselfish by buying him things.

The first week he wrapped it around a pole at high speed and killed his buddy — the consequence of giving a hostile boy a fast car! We used that as a warning.

"If you're angry and hostile at the world, you can't use the car. You can't have it just because it's your turn.

"Around here, only friendly people get the car."

Not being able to drive the car became one of the consequences of being angry.

If you don't teach your children about consequences, they have to learn when they are adults.

So, we let them suffer or enjoy the consequences of their choices. We point out examples of other children's good or bad consequences. And you supply your own consequences within your home life.

Here are some pertinent Bible verses:

Fathers, do not exasperate your children; instead, bring them up in the training and instruction of the Lord (Eph. 6:4).

My son, do not despise the Lord's *discipline* or be weary of his *reproof*, for the Lord reproves him whom he loves, as a father the son in whom he delights (Prov 3:11, 12).

The *rod* and *reproof* give wisdom, but a child left to himself brings shame to his mother (Prov. 29:15).

Discipline your son, and he will give you rest; he will give delight to your heart (Prov. 29:17).

Because sentence against an evil deed is not executed speedily, the heart of the sons of men is fully set to do evil (Eccl. 8:11).

There are some tough-sounding words in those verses:

chastening	reproof
correction	sentencing
	the rod

Then there are comforting words:

nurture and admonition of the Lord

love	wisdom
delight	rest

Here is an interesting mixture of words. This surely is not the picture of a mean, cruel, unkind adult venting his wrath on his children. On the contrary, here is a picture of someone familiar with the Word of God approaching a child whom he loves and delights in. His objective is to teach and to guide.

But when does physical punishment come in? That's the question you've been waiting for me to answer, isn't it? This question must be viewed within the framework of the limits you have set up. You are not taking your child by surprise. The limits are clear. As I see it, the pressure you use should move from weak to strong:

1. If there is any doubt about a child's knowledge of the limits, then, of course, instruction is in order.

2. If there is deliberate dawdling or loafing, some reproof may work.

3. Taking a child by the hand, picking it up, is still greater pressure.

4. Depriving a child of something meaningful may help.

5. Making something available that would reward a child may help.

6. Physical pain may help.

As I see it, physical pain should be reserved for defiant, rebellious, conscious challenge of your leadership. It should settle the question of who is in charge.

In his book *Dare to Discipline* Dr. Dobson says that nothing brings a parent and child closer together than for the mother or father to win decisively after being defiantly challenged. I agree. Nothing builds respect for you like confirming your leadership.

Dr. Dobson suggests a device for using minor pain for helping a child want to cooperate:

> There is a muscle, lying snugly against the base of the neck. Anatomy books list it as the trapezius muscle, and when firmly squeezed, it sends little messages to the brain saying, "This hurts; avoid recurrences at all costs." The pain is only temporary; it can cause no damage.[1]

A switch across the legs or a firm swat on the bottom will also help center their attention. How much pressure do you use? As little as possible, but enough to make happen what should happen.

Caution . . . pressure should be applied by friendly hands, but use it as often as necessary.

It is most important to be clear on this; if you love your children, you will chasten them. You do it, not because you lose your temper, but for the child's good — for his own personal development. It is taking a long look at his life, so that in the long run he will be happy.

When our children were preschoolers, they taught me a lesson in the relationship of physical pain to chastening. I would lie on my back, get a child up on my feet, boost him through the air to land on the couch. The children just loved it. This was a nightly ritual at our house. But one night one of the children missed the couch and came crashing to the floor. I thought the child would be injured. To my surprise, the child jumped up, eyes shining, and said:

[1] James Dobson, *Dare to Discipline* (Tyndale House: Wheaton, Illinois, 1971) pp. 35 and 38.

"Do it again, Daddy."

The other children added:

"Do it to me, too."

I experimented a bit that night, and deliberately threw the children on the floor. They roughhoused with each other. I even slapped their hands.

They loved it and wanted more.

A few days later, however, one of the children did something wrong. I grabbed the child's hand and spanked it with less force than several nights before. The child cried as if his heart would break.

What was the difference between several nights before and now? It was the emotional climate. A few nights before both of us were in a good mood and were having a good time. Now the mood was different. Physical pain does not necessarily mean punishment.

Has your child ever come home proudly bearing a black eye?

"I got it playing football!" Do you see how important the emotional climate is?

Some people think that if they never lay a hand on their child, they have not been cruel to them. Let's take a second look at this thinking. We all know about the pain of sharp words. You would not throw a brick at your child, but you might take a well-chosen sentence and let him have it. Sometimes a parent can hurt her child as much with a certain tone of voice as a spanking

Sometimes in your homes no one says a word. No one is laying a hand on anyone else. There is just silence, quietness — you are being ignored, tuned out. Such silence can be more painful than if you were to strike your child.

Punishment and physical pain need not be related. You can pick up your little baby, as some people do, and kindly pat him on the bottom. You're saying:

"I like you."

You walk up to a friend and slap him on the back, meaning:

"I like you."

Discipline and spanking need not imply a lack of

love. One of the reasons so many people abhor spanking is because they are angry when they do it.

The spirit in which it is done makes the difference. The use of physical punishment need not mean a lack of love. It just gets their attention. And not using physical punishment does not always mean love.

A cold shoulder can be just as painful as a slap. If you spank your child it must be done in a kindly, compassionate, tender way. Can you spank a child tenderly? Compassionately? You had better not spank him at all if you cannot.

The Lord disciplines and chastens you not because He lost His temper, but because He loves you. My concept of love is as it is described in 1 Corinthians 13. Love

> is patient . . . is kind . . . does not envy . . . does not boast . . . is not proud . . . is not rude . . . is not self-seeking . . . is not easily angered . . . keeps no record of wrongs . . . does not delight in evil, but rejoices in the truth. It always protects, always trusts, always hopes, always perseveres.

When you discipline your children, you should be doing it because they need it, not because you lost your temper. If you are out of control, do not blame the child. Get yourself under control before you approach a child.

These are important factors to remember as you develop consequences of your own to guide your children.

The Humming Physician

Attitude and viewpoint is important when a parent gets into this matter of making sure a child experiences the consequences — good or bad — of his actions.

I remember my team physician in high school. He had examined me many times and knew perfectly well that my physical condition was good.

Then, I developed a bad knee which swelled up so much that it filled my pantleg and hurt so much I couldn't straighten it up. So I hobbled into his office with my sore knee. Mind you, I'm in good shape otherwise, and he knows it. Yet, he didn't even mention my good physical condition. All he was interested in was my sore knee.

165

"Put it on this table and straighten it out."

Man, that was excrutiating pain.

Next, he began to thump it. He wanted to find out where it hurt the worst. So he thumped the sorest spot a few more times just to make sure he had it located.

Then he smiled at me and said:

"I've got to lance it."

So he's humming to himself as he goes off. When he returns — with a knife in his hand — he's smiling.

"This will hurt," he says.

Sure enough, he cut my knee open, lanced it and sewed it back up — all the time smiling, jovial. Then he said to me, obviously pleased with himself:

"There . . . now you'll get better."

At the time I was in horrible pain. I'd never had anything in my life that was sorer than that knee. Yet, the doctor was telling me that things were going to be all right. And smiling about it.

But it did. It got better.

Now isn't it strange that a surgeon is one of the most respected and highly paid people in the community. We don't like what he does. But we like the results, even if pain is involved. He is not cruel, but compassionately helpful.

As in parenthood, it's not what you do. It's the result of what you do. Consequences should produce results in the future. Don't be afraid to see that your children get the consequences — good and bad — of their behavior.

The Mystery of It All

There's a mystery to the entire process of working with your children. The matter of dealing with resistance. The matter of help. Respect. Supervision. Limits.

You must have a plan and then throw all you've got into following that plan . . . making sure the consequences for a child's behavior are there.

Several years ago, a couple was having a real problem with their thirteen-year-old son. He was flunking at school, fighting with his teachers, sassing his parents, fighting with his neighbors.

166

His parents tried everything.

First, they ignored him. Then they praised him. Then they rewarded him. Then they reasoned with him. Lectured him. Withheld dessert. Took his bike away. Made him stay in the house. Spanked him.

Nothing seemed to work. But the parents kept after the boy — all with that attitude of respect for him and constantly showing real affection and approval of the boy himself. They also prayed for patience and grace.

This went on for six months and nothing seemed to happen. Then, just as mysteriously as the behavior began, the boy began to change for the better.

Before, the boy had been condemned and censored by teachers, neighbors, Sunday school teachers.

Two years later, the same boy was a top student, on the football team, praised and admired by the coach, classmates, teachers, and neighbors.

This is the perfect picture of a dedicated, friendly set of parents seeking to train up a child in the way he should go. They realized it was a twenty-year process. Their concern was the process, not the decision of the moment. They had to hang loose and act by faith.

Trust Yourself /

Often when parents talk about their children who are in trouble, I ask them what they should have done instead of just leaving their children to themselves. In nearly every case, if the parents had done what they thought they should have done, they would have done what I would have recommended.

Many parents don't have confidence in their own ability. They need to trust themselves. They need to go with their own instincts, training — their plan.

Any two dedicated parents who are running the family business as friendly parents walking in the Spirit have sense enough to make good judgments.

The main job: Train them up in the way they should go. You have twenty years to mellow and mature. By then your children will want to be like you.

As we said before . . . let's have fun.

12 / Uh . . . Oh! What's Next?

12 / Uh . . . Oh! What's Next?

"Kids Say the . . . .

. . . darndest things." That's what Art Linkletter used to point out on his television show during his regular feature when he would interview a group of children.

And any parent with a sense of humor will have to agree. Sometimes what they say startles you and leaves you speechless because of the simplicity and honesty of it:

"Why are you so fat?" a little four-year-old asked a huge lady who tipped the scale at 250 pounds.

"Cause I eat too much," came the answer.

"Well, why don't you stop it, then?"

The fat lady was speechless. Just about as speechless as a smoker in a restaurant who was reprimanded by my granddaughter in a chilling way:

"You know," she said very sympathetically as she studied his dangling cigarette in horror, "if you keep smoking, you'll die."

They are also very unpredictable. Study a cute, angelic-looking little three-year-old face too long and you can forget how ornery little children can be.

The preacher at our church was standing by the door one day, greeting all those who had attended, when along came a mom and her little toddler, who could be best described as looking like the little princess out of a book.

171

Her Easter outfit made her even more angelic-looking as she walked squinting into the sunlight. And her mother was bursting with pride over her adorable-looking child.

"Oh, don't you look cute," said the pastor reaching down and tweaking the girl on the cheek. Unfortunately, he mistakenly tweaked too hard. The girl pulled back with a frown:

"Get your filthy hands off me."

When you expect your children to make an impression they may take you by surprise.

What Did You See at the Museum?

And one of the great all-time classic stories about coping with the fatigue of parenthood came from a woman from California, who told me this one.

"Resting on a chair in the local museum, I noticed a young couple with two small children. They sat down beside me, obviously weary after a hard day of being tourists.

" 'You go on up to the next floor and see what you want to, honey, and I'll stay here with the kids,' said the husband gallantly. As she went off, he stretched his legs out and smiled, happy to act as a sit-down baby-sitter.

"A few minutes later I went to the ladies' room, and there, to my surprise, was the wife, peacefully lying on a couch. She gave me a grin and a wink, then closed her eyes with a grateful sigh." She had outsmarted her husband that time.

The Take-Charge Parent

A relaxed approach seems to be the best way to handle a crisis. I know of one dad who was in the living room reading his paper, trying his best to block out an increasing uproar coming from the kitchen where two of the children were supposed to be helping Mother.

The argument seemed to be getting out of control. One child, especially, was screaming and protesting.

Mumbling "Why doesn't my wife do something," the father finally bolted from his chair and strode into the

172

kitchen, determined to show his wife how discipline should be carried out.

He grabbed a protesting boy by the arm and started whaling away, all the time ignoring the boy's attempted pleas of innocence. Having finished his stern discipline, he turned to his wife:

"I hope I put him into his place. He'll listen to you the next time."

Just as the father was about to walk back to his living room easy chair, he was stopped by a knowing look in his wife's eye.

"What's wrong?" he growled. "Didn't I spank him hard enough?"

"Oh, yes, you spanked him plenty hard. It's just that you spanked the wrong boy."

The same type of incident victimized a mother who acted hastily without accurate information. Her two boys were playing under the favorite tree in the front yard.

David, the older boy, advanced on Kevin, the younger, flashing his best outlaw scowl. His right hand, with the thumb sticking straight up, and the index finger pointed at Kevin formed the traditional shape of a gun.

"I'm gonna kill you," he growled, Cagney style. David was playing, but to Kevin it seemed that his life was in the balance. He reached down, hoisted a branch up in the air and brought it crashing down on the stickup man's head.

The surprised "gunman" started screaming bloody murder. When mother heard the screaming, she came shooting out the front door.

"Kevin hit me with a tree," the boy sobbed, running to his mother. The mother's discipline was quick, a hard spanking meted out to a boy without even giving him a chance to plead self-defense. Don't we do the dumbest things sometimes?

"I'm Learning to Fly"

My grandson went sweeping past his dad, complete with Superman cape and a determined look in his eye.

"Where are you going?"

"I'm going to learn how to fly."

173

"Oh," was all Dad had to say as Timmie burst into the bedroom and started climbing up to the top bunk.

The next sound Dad heard was a shattering crash. After a few minutes, the door opened slowly, and a wounded, ruffled boy staggered through the door, clutching his heel.

"Did you learn how to fly?" Dad asked.

"Yes," the boy said, keeping his pride high.

"Well, then, what happened to your heel?"

Timmie was momentarily stumped, his mind groping for a face-saving comment. Suddenly, his eyes lit up.

"My flying's all right," he said. "It's just that my landings aren't so good, yet."

Brushie, Brushie, Brushie/

I was a guest in a home one morning and awoke when a nasty voice yelled out:

"Nancy, you come here right now. This is ridiculous. You get up here."

Later that day I was talking to my host and asked him why the anger so early in the morning. The man, who is a perfectionist, replied:

"My wife is so sloppy. She's always getting the various containers and tubes mixed up in the bathroom. Today, I brushed my teeth with her hair set gel."

I thought it was funny. But I added:

"That's not too much fun, but you should be able to live with that. That shouldn't have gotten you down."

Good advice on my part. But a few months later I started brushing my teeth only to have a horrible taste explode in my mouth.

I looked at the tube. It said *Vitapoint* on it. I was furious. I picked up the hair set and was just about ready to throw it down the hall and into my bedroom, when I realized:

It's easier to give advice than to follow it.

A Girl and Her Dog /

Nancy was too small to properly handle the family dog, a large, black, shaggy but lovable mutt. One day the

174

dog came through the kitchen, with Nancy draped around his neck, feet dragging in desperation on the tile.

"Where are you taking Charlie?" the mother asked.

"I don't know yet," she replied. "But when he makes up his mind where he wants to go, I'm gonna take him there!"

Would you say that this proves that children need direction?

Geyser in the Bathroom /

Parent-child progress is a lurching bus at best. And perspective is everything. This is especially true in the area of toilet training, where a mother might best adopt as her slogan: "To dream the impossible dream."

But every now and then there is a breakthrough. I have a friend who works at home, and his study is right next to the children's bathroom. For several weeks, the mother had been trying to get their eighteen-month-old child to produce something.

Then, suddenly, one morning when my friend was having a meeting with three other writers, there were a series of excited knocks on the study door. He ran to the door and opened it.

In dashed the little girl — the last of the streakers. She stopped suddenly, taking stock of all the people who were in the usually deserted study. Finally, she figured out which was her dad.

"Come, quick, Daddy. Come and see the potty."

Embarrassed, the father hustled into the adjoining bathroom where his wife was doubled up with laughter. As his daughter pointed at the potty, he saw that it was empty and completely bone-dry.

His wife then told him that the little girl had been sitting on the potty chair when she suddenly had been surprised by a little, almost inaudible, gas explosion from underneath.

That little explosion had triggered all the excitement.

Michael's case was a little more dramatic, al-

175

though just as significant. For weeks, Michael's mom had made several daily trips to the bathroom and would sit (Remember: "They also serve who only sit and wait"?) on the edge of the bathtub in a vigil, waiting for that magical moment when Michael would finally put the little potty chair to use.

On this particular day, Michael had gotten pretty bored with the whole affair and was lolling and slumping on the chair, when suddenly a geyser of urine shot straight up in the air . . . over the rug . . . into the sink . . . and even on a surprised but now very alert mother.

Mommy was aghast. Not Michael. He was oblivious to everything but the success of the moment.

He kept jumping up and down and pointing at the two or three drops that somehow did go into the potty.

"Look, Mommy. Look! Look! Look!" he kept exclaiming, while jumping up and down.

For Michael's mother, it was mixed emotions all the way.

Conversations of a Child

Albert always wondered what children talk about when they are just getting to know each other. Then one day, he found out.

A cousin was visiting. She was seven years old and so was Albert's son. On the way home from the train station, there was silence for a long time. Then, all of a sudden, Albert's son turned to his cousin and asked:

"Lost any teeth lately?"

Taking on Grandma

Two grandchildren appeared out of the basement; each one just about hidden behind a big, wide pillow. All grandma could see was two sets of little arms.

"Where are you going?" she asked.

"Outside to play," two little voices replied in unison from behind the pillows. They were absolutely confident that grandma would grant their request and stood there flabbergasted when she turned them down. So they struggled back down the stairs with the big pillows. Pretty soon, up came Matt, saying:

"Mellyn is downstairs, and she says that if we can't take those pillows outside, she's gonna be mad."

Well, he didn't get anywhere with grandma. So in whipped-dog fashion, he plodded back downstairs. After awhile, grandma heard footsteps. Here came Matt, who again was acting as a spokesman for Mellyn.

" . . . and Mellyn says if we can't take those pillows outside, she won't eat." Matt got turned down and trudged back downstairs.

In a few minutes he appeared again, saying: "Mellyn says if we can't take those pillows outside, she won't sleep."

But all this got for poor Matt was the same answer from grandma. Pretty soon, grandma heard two sets of footsteps coming up the stairs. When they appeared they were just about hidden again by these two big, wide pillows.

Now Mellyn spoke up with a gleam in her eye.

"We're gonna go outside with these pillows anyway." Two little children, ready to take on the establishment. But, alas, they got turned around and headed back downstairs by grandma.

Those Aren't My Boots!

One mother tells this story. She went to pick up her son after school one day at kindergarten. When she went in, her son burst into tears.

"Mommy, there's only one pair of boots left in the hall and they aren't mine."

Assuming the child knew what he was talking about, Mom and the boy's teacher searched under the desks and in corners but could find no other boots. Exhausted, Mom finally went out into the hall, and there were her son's boots.

Exasperated, she called her son and said gruffly, "These are your boots."

"Oh, no. They can't be my boots. Mine had snow on them," the little boy replied.

A Closing Statement /

The junior high boy was asked what he wanted to be when he grew up.

"A writer."

"Would you like to have a family, with children of your own?"

"Yes, I would like that."

Then, he paused for a moment, for he had just come through a rather serious disagreement with his parents the day before. And he had lost the debate.

"I'd like to take that back. I'd like to have my own children. But I'd rather not be a . . . you know . . . a parent."

We're sure he will change his mind. But we hope that when he does become a parent someday, he will be one who has a sense of humor and looks on parenthood the way we feel it should be.

Enjoyable!

13 / A Baker's Dozen . . . for Parents

13 / A Baker's Dozen . . . for Parents

Hey, I Heard That One Before!/

We hope that's what you'll be saying as you read this chapter, for it's time to look back at the last twelve chapters and remind ourselves of the principles in this book. As you reconsider these principles, consider them as more than just words — consider them as thirteen friends who can help make parenthood more enjoyable.

With a Little Help . . . From Thirteen Friends!/

1. *Confident expectation* — based on the assumption that you are doing or requiring something you believe is worthwhile and in the best interests of your child. If you are, you will have enough conviction to see it through.

2. *You need help from a source outside yourself* – God Himself, through Jesus Christ. "If only my child would behave, then I would be happy."

The good news is that happiness comes from God, and neither people or circumstances can interfere.

> But the fruit of the spirit is love, joy, peace, patience, kindness, goodness, faithfulness, gentleness, self-control; against such things there is no law (Gal. 5:22,23, NASB).

3. *Parenthood is a partnership.* The basic job of parenthood is to design a harness both of you will wear.

Make my joy complete by being of the same mind, maintaining the same love, united in spirit, intent on one purpose. Do nothing from selfishness or empty conceit, but with humility of mind let each of you regard one another as more important than himself (Phil. 2:2,3, NASB).

4. *But the nature of human nature is to go your own way.*

All of us like sheep have gone astray, each of us has turned to his own way; but the LORD has caused the iniquity of us all to fall on Him (Isaiah 53:6, NASB).

In all our dealings, whether it involves your partner . . . or your children . . . or your best friend . . . the relationship will tend to strain at the point of decision making.

5. *The husband is the president* — and is responsible for making sure he and his wife wear the harness they both designed.

Be subject to one another in the fear of Christ. Wives, be subject to your own husbands, as to the Lord (Eph. 5:21, 22, NASB).

When decision making leads to a stalemate, the husband settles it. This is the key to it all.

6. *The wife is the executive vice-president* — and usually the leading expert on the home and family. In her role as such, she needs to have clear-cut responsibilities with appropriate authority.

7. *Both parents must be effectively busy.* Proverbs 31 describes the talents of a woman. It's a creative job to make sure both parents are using their talent in or out of the home. Jesus gives a formula for greatness:

Whoever wishes to become great among you shall be your servant (Mark 10:43, NASB).

8. *Parenthood is a twenty-year process.* It's a long haul. Longsuffering *with* joy are fruits of the Spirit. You pull off a few perfect plays, but mostly it's daily effort and keeping at it for twenty years.

9. *Setting the limits is the parents' responsibility.*

The boundaries and rules (called limits in this book) are the result of adult decision, not a child's.

> Train up a child in the way he should go, even when he is old he will not depart from it (Prov. 22:6, NASB).

It's a family plan, one that keeps changing. Therefore, many meetings between parents are necessary to keep an up-to-date, reasonable plan.

10. *Resistance to the plan is normal . . . so your children need your help.* The nature of human nature is to go your own way. Children have a plan of their own, so resistance to your plan can be expected. They need a good-humored mother who appreciates the contest and enjoys it, and a good-humored father who backs her up and steps in to help. Here are some tools to help you overcome their resistance:

  a. Redirecting a child's behavior or attention
  b. Giving physical help as needed
  c. Giving more help than needed
  d. Preparing in advance
  e. Use pressure from weak to strong

The use of these tools is a matter of your judgment, a matter of making a friendly executive decision.

11. *Children need supervision* in setting limits, dealing with resistance, giving help. Put them together and give them a name. That name is supervision. It is commitment to the same limits and personal involvement in making them work. Your style may differ, but the limits remain the same. You gotta believe! In your plan!

12. *The truth about consequences.* Choices have their consequences — good or bad, comfortable or uncomfortable, painful or pleasant. Announcing the consequences for a child's choices and making them happen is a crucial part of learning.

> Do not be deceived. God is not mocked; for whatever a man sows, this he will also reap (Gal. 6:7, NASB).

13. *Trust your own instincts.* I'll put my hopes on the judgment of any parents who walk in the Spirit, respect

183

one another and their children, and are committed to a mutually agreeable and mutually binding plan.

Let's Have a Ball!

And our most consistent theme in this entire book is that parenthood can be fun. Parenthood should be a twenty-year adventure, not a twenty-year sentence.

Get that outside help from God, personalize those friendly principles into your life. And let's have some fun.

That's the way we're going to end this book — by having a little more fun!